coaching in the library

P9-CFB-935

ALA Editions purchases fund advocacy, awareness, and accreditation programs for library professionals worldwide.

Coaching in the Library

a management strategy for achieving excellence

SECOND EDITION

RUTH F. METZ

AMERICAN LIBRARY ASSOCIATION • CHICAGO 2011

RUTH METZ is a consultant, coach, and trainer specializing in library management, organizational development, and leadership development. Her firm, Ruth Metz Associates (www.librarycoach.com), specializes in helping community and library leaders as they plan, manage, and develop their libraries. Metz is a librarian and coach with many years of practical management experience in libraries and public agencies. She coaches library leaders, managers, and boards as well as other public sector managers and governing bodies. Through coaching, consulting, and training, Metz helps clients develop a coaching culture in their organizations.

© 2011 by the American Library Association. Any claim of copyright is subject to applicable limitations and exceptions, such as rights of fair use and library copying pursuant to Sections 107 and 108 of the U.S. Copyright Act. No copyright is claimed in content that is in the public domain, such as works of the U.S. government.

Printed in the United States of America
15 14 13 12 11   5 4 3 2 1

While extensive effort has gone into ensuring the reliability of the information in this book, the publisher makes no warranty, express or implied, with respect to the material contained herein.

ISBN-13: 978–0-8389–1037–5

Library of Congress Cataloging-in-Publication Data
Metz, Ruth F.
  Coaching in the library : a management strategy for achieving excellence / Ruth F.
Metz. -- 2nd ed.
      p. cm.
  Includes bibliographical references and index.
  ISBN 978-0-8389-1037-5 (alk. paper)
  1. Library personnel management--United States. 2. Mentoring in library science--
United States. I. Title.
  Z682.2.U5M48 2010
  023'.9--dc22
                                                          2010027235

Cover design by Karen Sheets de Gracia
Text design in Berkeley, Scala Sans, and Gotham by Adrianna Sutton

♾ This paper meets the requirements of ANSI/NISO Z39.48-1992 (Permanence of Paper).

ALA Editions also publishes its books in a variety of electronic formats.
For more information, visit the ALA Store at www.alastore.ala.org and select eEditions.

SEP 1 7 2015

Z
682.2
U5M48
2011

contents

acknowledgments

I AM THANKFUL to the American Library Association for inviting a second edition of *Coaching in the Library*. My consulting and coaching work over the last several years has further clarified coaching's significance as a multifaceted tool for professional and organizational development. I am awed at my good fortune at having so many interesting, challenging, and inspiring teachers: my clients, associates, colleagues, and friends. This edition is an opportunity to "give back" and to appeal to library leaders to work toward ever more effective library organizations.

introduction

COACHING is a multidimensional concept. That is, it has many possible applications on many different levels. Thus, the full meaning of coaching can be grasped only by understanding its purpose, which varies from situation to situation. In general, however, coaching is the purposeful and skillful effort by one individual to help another achieve specific performance goals. Whether the coach is working with an individual or group (the "player"), she facilitates the player's attainment of the player's goals. The success of this effort depends on the cooperation of both parties. The player is willing to be challenged, supported, and influenced by the coach. The coach enables this willingness throughout the stages of coaching.

Coaching is an important organizational tool because people in today's workforce at every level constantly have to work on the interface of their knowledge, skills, and experience in a changing and somewhat unpredictable environment. Coaching is not just something that engages people's efficiency. It increases individual and organizational effectiveness through changing times. Coaching has a multiplier effect. It enhances the library's assets. The more able the individual is to dynamically apply his skills to an ever-changing environment, the more valuable he is to the organization.

WHY DO LIBRARIES NEED COACHING?

The greatest challenge to library leaders is to enable their organizations to continuously adapt to this ever-changing, ever more complex environment. For while it is hard to imagine a more exciting time for libraries, it is nevertheless a time of many, many challenges. Coaching in libraries is more important than ever for helping our organizations and the individuals who lead them and work in them.

For instance, library leaders know they need to lead the continuous redevelopment of libraries. Yet many believe that they do not have the organizational capacity to go about structuring and successfully implementing what libraries urgently need: the evolution of twenty-first-century service, organizational, and funding models. The ability to effectively tackle such institutional challenges is fundamental to the success of leaders and the survival of libraries.

The main reason to integrate coaching into library organizations is to enable these institutions to successfully adapt to the changes they face. People in today's workforce at every level constantly have to work on the interface of their knowledge, skills, and experience in a changing and somewhat unpredictable environment. The coach plays a key role by being the "outside" person who has no bias, no agenda, other than to help the individual adjust her already valuable skills in a dynamic world. Coaching assumes that there is no limit to how effective a person or an organization can become.

Coaching provides time to step back and reflect on one's own behavior and influence. "Reflective practice" is a part of the learning process and has become an important feature of professional training programs in many disciplines.[1] For most people, real reflective practice needs another person, such as a coach, who can ask appropriate questions so that the reflection is objective.

People who work in libraries are not only constantly faced with knowledge gaps in changing technology, but also with how to manage the integration of the technology into their ongoing work. The walls around the library are not as solid as they once were. Less than a decade ago, the staffing structure and titles were set and staid. The work of libraries today calls for a much more diverse array of knowledge, skills, and abilities than ever before. The expectation is for more flexibility. Library workers are constantly being expected to do what they were not expected to do before. People who work in libraries have to be constantly learning and adapting to new technologies and working in collaboration with others.

At the same time that technology is changing the work of libraries, other factors are impacting the volatility of the workplace. For example, the competition among the different generations of library workers has become intense. The library workforce spans three generations: the Baby Boomers, Generation X, and Generation Y. The current economic downturn has kept many aging Baby Boomers in the workforce, and has also resulted in fewer new jobs. There is a sense of frustration and even resentment that these older workers have not made room for the younger generations. People of color represent a progressively larger proportion of the

workforce, and this will continue to grow. Global migration will continue to diversify the workforce. The mix of various perspectives and values in the future library workplace will contrast dramatically to the more homogeneous workplace of the last thirty years.

Individuals in the library workforce are also facing very challenging work-life decisions. Many who planned to leave are staying on because of the economic downturn. The care of children, the elderly, and the disabled are straining workers' capacity to work full time and to make ends meet. The International Coach Federation's (ICF's) "2009 Global Coaching Client Study" reports that 36 percent of coaching clients put work-life balance as one of the top three motivators for seeking coaching.[2] Meanwhile, some librarians who were recruited into the profession with the promise that there would be jobs as the Baby Boomer generation retired in great numbers are leaving by the side exits for other careers.[3] These conditions mean the need for coaching is ever-present and increasing.

WHAT IS HAPPENING WITH COACHING IN GENERAL?

Libraries are not alone in these challenges. The global coaching industry is one of the fastest growing in the world. The ICF, with over 16,000 members in over 90 countries, has had a 645 percent increase in membership since 1999. It certifies coaches: nearly 1,200 in 2007, a sixfold increase over the 200 certified in 2004. Over 14,000 articles on coaching were published in 2008, a 52 percent increase over 2007.

Coaching has become more accessible to more people. The taxonomy of coaching categories has expanded with the market: life, career, career transition, enjoyment, family, finances, grief, health, job, leadership development, management, parenting, personal, relationship, spiritual, and a variety of other specialties. The forms or modes of coaching are changing as well. Face-to-face coaching is being supplemented with telephone and Internet coaching.

Where once coaching was for the business elite, the benefits of coaching are now well known and dispersed across industries and throughout organizations, penetrating into all levels of the workplace. The role of coaching as perceived by leaders has grown. Furthermore, the application of coaching has become more strategic, with organizations integrating coaching with other learning experiences, developmental processes, and internal human resources (HR) processes. There is growing organizational demand for leadership development systems that prepare tomorrow's leaders. The changing workforce is apt to challenge long-standing norms that affect how emergent leaders develop as leaders. Coaching can play a significant role in showing the way.

Research supports the thesis that coaching, developing others, and giving feedback are critical skills of effective leaders. Yet these skills are often rated by chief executives among the lowest.[4] Despite this, many organizations today expect their executives to be "leader coaches." Leader coaches are executives who are intentional about developing direct reports, peers, and emergent leaders and, accordingly, their own skills for coaching. Many organizations have adopted the ability to coach direct reports and peers as a core competency for their chief executives.

There is a growing expectation in both the private and public sectors for organizational leaders to integrate coaching into their organizations. Organizations are developing a practice of coaching: building communities of coaches, integrating coaching with performance systems and development processes, and applying coaching to organizational initiatives.

Many organizations are moving from individual leadership development to collective leadership development. That is, it isn't only the leader but the leadership team, the management team, and the cross-functional team that develop their collective leadership capacity. Organizations are integrating coaching with other learning practices. They are building their internal coaching capacity. This takes the form of classroom instruction and skills practice, shadow coaching, ongoing workshops, and individual coaching that help the coach improve his coaching. Organizations are combining internal and external coaching, accessing the variety of specializations and expertise, and building a cadre of coaches that they can easily access.[5]

In effect, organizations are creating a new norm in organizational learning and, in the process, developing a culture of coaching. The evolution of coaching in organizations is toward greater normalcy and transparency. This new paradigm is superseding the more compartmentalized and elit-ist approach of the past. It is creating cultures of coaching within organizations and dialogue about coaching within the organization's community of coaches. In these communities of coaching, people are developing a shared vocabulary and knowledge where concepts, approaches, and ideas can be discussed and resources shared. The practice of coaching is having a cascading effect throughout organizations, increasing the effectiveness and efficiency of both individuals and teams.

There is at present an emphasis in the coaching industry on quantifying the return on investment (ROI). Organizations want to know what they are getting for their expenditures on executive coaching, in particular. This is a difficult task because the bottom line is generally influenced by many factors and often indirectly by the CEO's behaviors and performance.

An overemphasis on quantitative measures can underestimate what the client has learned or can focus too narrowly on his development. However, in coaching, measuring results is crucial because it tells a person what he has accomplished as the result of coaching and enables him to examine the effect of his performance on the organization.

The conversation about results begins at the start of the coaching relationship and is revisited throughout. Results are generally measured in terms of behavioral change, performance improvement, and service improvement. Service improvement is often difficult to tie directly to coaching because many factors can be at play. In general, measuring results is done through formal self-assessment, informal feedback from stakeholders, and formal feedback obtained through surveys and other instruments.

WHAT IS HAPPENING WITH COACHING IN LIBRARIES?

Today, there is a different foundation in the library industry for coaching compared to just a few years ago. People who are developing their careers in libraries and newcomers to the library workplace are familiar with the concept of coaching. In their education and training, they have been encouraged to think positively about coaching for themselves and their organizations. Many are more ready and more inclined to be introspective about their role in the workplace and to accept the need for constant adaptability. They are aware of the benefits of coaching. Their friends and associates in and out of the library have had direct exposure to coaching. Coaching is more and more recognized in the library world and is more accepted as standard practice.

There is a growing readiness and expectation for coaching in today's library workplace. For example, the Urban Libraries Council's Executive Leadership Institute (ELI) program graduated seventy-five "fellows" between 2001 and 2005.[6] Executive coaching and reflective practice were part of the program. These are some of the new leaders stepping into executive positions around the country.

One of the ELI fellows and now the director of a large metropolitan library says she became an advocate for coaching in libraries after experiencing it both in the ELI program and in her workplace. She said she became a convert because coaching helped her develop her effectiveness as a leader through several successive, increasingly responsible promotions within her organization. Now she elects coaching for herself, encourages it for her management team and staff, and budgets for it. Coaching was also a component of a 2007 Institute of Library and Museum Services grant to help fund the recruitment, matriculation, and early career development of 150 minority students in master's-level library and information studies programs.[7]

These alumni are bringing coaching and reflective practice into library organizations with them as their careers advance. Workshops and online courses have introduced coaching as a concept in libraries. For example, California's InfoPeople library staff training program introduced coaching in libraries in 2003 and has continued to feature programs that build coaching skills. Dynix Institute's online training programs have also featured coaching. Several national library leadership development programs feature mentoring and coaching.

While there is a growing awareness and use of coaching in some libraries, its use is still not widespread. Furthermore, its use is generally not strategically focused on improving the overall effectiveness of library organizations.

HOW CAN LIBRARIES USE COACHING?

It is time for library leaders to think about coaching as more than a tool for their own development, improving substandard performance in others, or

developing a leadership bench. We have to get away from the idea that all coaching is problem-solving and that you call in a coach when a problem needs to be corrected.

It is time to become purposeful about the application of coaching on a broad scale. Library leaders can authorize and influence the development of a "coaching system" in their organizations that supports the learning and development of individuals and the organization as a whole. A coaching system can in turn be integrated into ongoing "systems" such as learning, performance management, and leadership development.

Integrating coaching wisely into the organization begins with intentionality and an understanding of organizational need. Intentionality means that the library leader makes the case for an integration of coaching practice into organizational development efforts in response to a set of identified needs. She authorizes it and is involved in its design and its evolution.

In the midst of the current severe economic downturn when budgets are strained, readers may dismiss the notion of integrating coaching into their organizations as unaffordable, impractical, or both. However, the economic downturn is all the more reason to use coaching. Typically, library organizations are spending 65 percent or more of their budget on personnel. Coaching leverages human capital.

Libraries can afford coaching by purposefully cultivating coaching behaviors in their workforce. For example, coaching behaviors and skills can be developed in the library's leader, in managers and supervisors, and in the library's human resources department. Work units and teams can learn coaching behaviors and apply them with one another. A library can develop a cadre of internal coaches whose work portfolio includes selected coaching assignments. The library's core competencies for new hires can include coaching, and the library's new personnel appointments can be made accordingly.

The library can use external coaches for assignments that the organization itself cannot fulfill. External coaches may be available through a parent organization or an exchange arrangement with a peer institution. It is likely that the organization is already allocating funds in HR and other units for a variety of personnel learning activities, including conferences, workshops, training, and supervision. Leaders should insist that these modes channel learning that is aligned with initiatives for developing a more effective organization.

The effort needed will vary from library to library. Some library organizations may be well positioned for development while others are not. Working on the organization is not an all-or-nothing proposition. Library leaders, however, must take the long view. Just as they are grappling with service models of the future, they must also grapple with what library organizations of the future must be. These two dimensions of the library are interdependent.

WHAT DOES STRATEGIC COACHING LOOK LIKE?

Imagine you are the director of a library whose operating costs are rising at a higher rate than its revenues. Costs are rising by 10 percent per year while revenues are increasing by 3 percent per year. The deficit is largely structural; that is, it is ongoing and will continue to grow, because it is largely driven by fixed obligations. For example, the library is contractually obligated to a salary schedule, salary increases or cost of living adjustments, retirement contributions as a percentage of compensation, and health care premiums. These costs are growing at 15 percent per year. Meanwhile, other operating costs such as telecommunications, utilities, office supplies, vendor contracts, interdepartmental charges from the parent jurisdiction, and so forth are also growing, at an overall rate of 6 percent.

The overall result is that it is costing more to operate the library each year than the library is receiving in revenues. A library may be fortunate to have built an operating reserve fund and it uses this for a few years to offset its structural deficit. Most libraries would not be in that position, and so they are forced to reduce hours, staffing, collections, and administrative and technical support in rounds as the revenue-to-expenses situation worsens. Even the library with a reserve fund eventually will succumb to these rounds of reductions.

When branch closures are proposed, the community becomes embroiled in a pitched battle over limited resources. To make matters worse, revenues in the next few years are expected to be reduced even further. While this takes place, the library is trying to introduce and apply new technology to serve the public. However, it is strapped for resources that its leaders and staff believe it needs to be responsive, competitive, and viable. The library needs to develop and contract at the same time.

The new library director believes that part of the solution is in developing new service models that can deliver today's and tomorrow's needed services and that cost less to provide. However, there are many obstacles to creating new service models. Some staff are resistant to change; managers and supervisors in some cases are overly concerned with appeasing staff and seem to have lost sight of community needs. The senior managers have never developed a sense of team leadership. They aren't skilled in working with staff to develop alternative service models. There is no organizational compass to give them bearings for designing new service models. Some managers will be retiring soon, but there is no apparent "bench" of aspiring leaders to follow them. The structural budget deficit has been managed with the use of reserve funds, and staff and the community have been unaware that operating costs are outstripping revenues. The economic downturn has further reduced revenues, adding urgency to the problem.

Strategic coaching for this organization would begin with the leader and then with the leader and executive team together. Several purposes would be served simultaneously. Coaching would help them establish a focus for organizational development while providing action learning for team leadership. They would also begin an organizational needs assessment and an overall strategy for developing the organization according to those needs: the need to develop new service models, to resolve the structural budget deficit, to engage staff, to develop succession leaders, and to help staff through change transitions, including their own career and work-life balance transitions.

This library would benefit from multidimensional coaching to

- Support the library director in clarifying and prioritizing executive direction
- Build executive, management, and team leadership capacity
- Facilitate the process of developing new service models and a sustainable budget
- Develop new leaders and a leadership bench
- Ensure success after promotions or new hires
- Develop coaching behaviors in the library director, managers, and supervisors
- Sustain effective individual and group performance

Whether the coaching is for individuals or groups, it has an overarching purpose to improve organizational effectiveness. Just as libraries have a strategic plan of service, they need a strategic plan for organizational development. Coaching strategically helps organizations respond to the reality of their situation. It is a process that requires time and multiple interactions.

When a library leader can influence the energies of the organization in a positive and progressive direction, the community will respond with its support. In the twenty-first century, libraries that cannot make and sustain this fundamental connection will not be sustained by the community.

HOW DO I FIND A COACH?

What Am I Looking for in a Coach?

Coaching has many dimensions and purposes. Finding the right coach begins with being able to describe as you see it the situation and the need. Think about and write down the need and what outcomes you would like to see. Also write down any particular requirements the situation may call for in the coach. Then you are in a position to talk about your needs with prospective coaches or with trusted colleagues for possible referrals.

For many, talking the situation over first with a confidant will help clarify the issues, the knowledge and skills needed, and the desired outcomes. In so doing, you hear yourself—sometimes for the first time—talk about the situation. If you are the library director, your confidant may be your deputy director, your HR director, or a library director colleague: someone in whom you can confide.

The give-and-take of your confidential conversation helps you clarify your own thoughts, as does the perspective of another trusted person. By clarifying your own thoughts, you will be better able to know what you are looking for in a coach and to target your search. You will also be better prepared to have an initial conversation with one or more prospective coaches.

The coach has to be a person that the individual or the group can trust in the sense that the coach is credible in an interpersonal way. The prospective coach who takes the position that he has all the answers and that the client is only there to listen to the coach is not credible in an interpersonal way. The coach shouldn't take the attitude that you've done everything wrong and now he'll tell you how to do it right.

A good coach comes in with an attitude that is respectful and recognizes that coaching is a balanced relationship. The coach's advice needs to be exactly tied to the real situation as the person or group sees it. The coach has to respect the breadth of knowledge and understanding of those inside the organization. A good coach takes time to assess the situation.

Where Do I Look for a Coach?

Coaches can be internal or external. If you have built coaching muscle within your organization, you can look internally first. Your human resources department or parent HR might be able to provide coaching or a referral. Some libraries have established a cadre of coaches—internal, external, or both—that they call into service as needed.

Finding a coach that specializes in libraries is difficult at this time. For example, at present, a Google search for library coaches will lead you to just one source: mine. However, there are library consultants who may fit the bill. The "Selected Resources" section of this book identifies library consultant search websites and a few additional resources to help you find coaches who are familiar with the library industry.

Several generic coaching industry websites offer free coach-finding and referral. The "Selected Resources" section of this book lists several coaching industry find-a-coach websites. Keep in mind that the search structures of coaching industry websites are geared toward the business sector rather than the public sector, at this time. Thus, at the time of this writing you wouldn't be able to search for coaches that specialize in libraries, academics, or schools. You will therefore have to be resourceful in your search.

As previously stated, the coaching industry is one of the fastest growing on the globe. According to an ICF spokesperson, there are over 120 training programs, and only 20 are accredited by the ICF. Establishing a credentialing program that has global credibility and holds value is at the top of the industry's priority list. The ICF, for example, is working to bring its certification program into compliance with the International Standards Organization's standards for bodies that certify persons. A spokesperson for the Institute for Professional

Excellence in Coaching said that the global market will need 100,000 coaches in the next five years to meet the expected demand. For some time, it will continue to be a buyer-beware market.

Given these conditions, referral through library industry channels is as viable an option as any for finding a coach. When you are not able to find a coach through referral and need to rely on a finding resource or the telephone book, it is advisable to limit your search to certified coaches.

Interview any prospective coaches. The interview, of course, should be directed at learning about them, their credentials and experience, and fees. Fees vary widely depending upon credentials and locale, from $60/hour to $400/hour. Packages for services over time are generally less expensive than an hourly rate.

In interviewing prospective coaches, be as interested in their questions as you are in their credentials and fees. A good prospect is someone who restates your need in a way that captures the essence of the issue. The interview should help you understand your need better than when you started. If the interview doesn't do that for you, keep looking.

For coaching to work, a person has to be willing to be coached. It has to be the right coach. The individual and the coach have to be clear about what they are doing. One of the reasons coaching fails is that people don't understand what it is. It is not therapy, though it may be therapeutic.

BEAUTIFUL POSSIBILITIES

Technology is enabling people, institutions, and organizations to share information and be creative in ways that are new and exciting. Libraries have played an important role in making the benefits of technology accessible to a broad base of people. Perhaps this is why public awareness and satisfaction with libraries is at an all-time high.

According to the American Library Association, an uncommissioned 2008 Harris poll found that almost all Americans say they view their local library as an important educational resource.[8] Seven out of ten agree that their local library is a pillar of the community, a community center, a family destination, and a cultural center. For many, many people, libraries have been a transformational force in their lives. It is this transformational quality that influences both library users and nonusers alike in supporting public funding for libraries.[9]

We know that it is a challenge of immense proportions for libraries to survive in the decades ahead. Their survival is as much a consequence of adaptable, flexible, and durable organizations as it is a matter of adapting services for an ever-changing marketplace. These are two sides of the same coin. You don't get one without the other.

Coaching by itself will not transform an organization. However, it is a powerful tool in helping individuals and groups in the organization to make the transitions that come with change. Change is a constant; it is a catalyst for more change. An organization that understands this and intentionally aids the workforce in making transitions will survive better than one that simply reacts to one change after another.

Coaching actively and willingly supports people in libraries as they learn. It is our consistency of interaction in the face of constant change that leads to stability, predictability, and a more durable workplace. This durability gives people a firm place to stand, even amidst constant change. It is the ultimate place from which to be consistently effective as an organization and community institution.

ABOUT THIS BOOK

One of the purposes of *Coaching in the Library* is to develop your sensitivity to conditions that threaten the effectiveness of your own library. This is accomplished through using many examples and presenting these in a variety of ways. The examples, scenarios, and applications are all paths in the book that lead to the same goal: to cultivate in you an observant attitude about what threatens performance and to help you get a feel for what constitutes superior performance.

The style and approach of this book are intended to help you envision an environment that you may never have experienced. This is also to suggest that the workplace environment is not simply imposed on you, but can be influenced for the better through an observant awareness of what threatens performance and through a conscious choice of actions.

The term *player* in this book refers to the person who is coached. The term *supervisor* is used generically. That is, it refers here not to a personnel classification but to the function of supervision. In this book, a supervisor can be the library director, a manager, a supervisor, a librarian, or any person who is responsible for formally evaluating the performance of another person in the library. Coaches can come from outside the library or from inside. Anyone inside the library organization with the willingness, skills, and abilities is a potential coach.

The basic approach used in this book is to describe and illustrate what it means to coach, why it is important to coach, and how to coach. Because coaching is a multidimensional concept, the examples and applications offer a range of situations, from simple to complex. This approach reinforces for the reader that every coaching situation is different. There is no "one" way, but there are many ways to make use of effective coaching behaviors. Modeling is the best teacher. The examples and applications in this book model coaching in practical library situations.

The chapter organization is essentially the same throughout the book. Each chapter is arranged in five sections: the prelude sets the scene, or context, for the chapter. It is followed by what, why, and how sections. To illustrate the how of coaching, the application at the end of the chapter applies one or more of the coaching concepts described in that chapter. For example, the chapter 1 application applies the coaching process framework (observation, diagnosis, prognosis, and treatment) to a coaching intervention.

Chapter 1 introduces the concept of performance factors, which include performance barriers and pathways to excellence. These are observational categories based on commonsense experience. All chapters describe how coaching can help cultivate pathways to excellence.

The scope of Coaching in the Library moves beyond how libraries typically use coaching. Chapter 1, "Coaching Overview," describes the basic structure of coaching. Chapter 2, "The Effective Coach," describes and illustrates basic coaching behaviors. Chapters 3, 4, 5, and 6 describe and illustrate coaching for individuals, teams, leaders, and managers, respectively. The chapters on coaching teams, leaders, and managers focus on what is distinctive about coaching these people. Chapter 7, "Coaching and Organizational Effectiveness," illustrates the role of coaching in library rejuvenation and transformation.

The intended audience includes library leaders, HR directors, managers, supervisors, and teams. In addition, this book will be of interest to any employee who serves as a team member, mentor, or peer coach and to anyone who functions in an informal coaching role with a coworker. It will also be of interest to individuals who are being coached or to those who are considering coaching others.

The overarching reason to coach is to gradually make the library more and more effective in serving its community. The library's *community* includes all those communities served by the library regardless of the library type: the communities of the academic library, public library, school library, and special library. Many people prefer to read about a subject in a familiar context; therefore, some of the examples in this book are set in a particular type of library. Mostly, they concern common library workplace experiences. After all, these work settings involve people, and coaching is about people.

The examples and applications in this book are based on over thirty years of experience and are rendered as composites of experiences. Any resemblance to individuals, organizations, or incidents is coincidental.

NOTES

1. Chris Argyris. Reflective practice is the ability to reflect on what you are about to do, what you are doing while you are doing it, and what you have done having done it.

2. International Coach Federation, "International Coach Federation 2009 Global Coaching Client Study," 2009.

3. From interview with Lorelle R. Swader, director, Office for Human Resource Development and Recruitment, American Library Association.

4. Corporate Leadership Council, *Voice of the Leader: A Quantitative Analysis of Leadership Bench Strength and Development Strategies* (Washington, DC: Corporate Executive Board, 2001).

5. Center for Creative Leadership, *The CCL Handbook of Coaching: A Guide for the Leader Coach*, ed. Sharon Ting and Peter Scisco (San Francisco: Jossey-Bass, 2006).

6. The Executive Leadership Institute program was extant in 2000–2003. It included a coaching component. See the "Executive Leadership Institute Evaluation Report" prepared by the Center for Creative Leadership for the Urban Libraries Council, September 2008, http://www.urbanlibraries.org/associations/9851/files/CCL_pub.pdf.

7. Under the 2007 Laura Bush 21st Century Librarian Program, the Institute of Museum and Library Services awarded the American Library Association a grant of $872,920 to help fund the recruitment, matriculation, and early career development of 150 minority students in master's-level library and information studies programs and to provide mentoring and coaching of 60 additional students from underrepresented backgrounds.

8. Harris Poll, ALA, 2008, http://www.ala.org/ala/newspresscenter/news/pressreleases2008/September2008/ORSharris.cfm.

9. OCLC report, "From Awareness to Funding: A Study of Library Support in America," 2008, http://www.oclc.org/reports/funding/default.htm.

1 coaching overview

PRELUDE

When I ask library employees to describe the work environment they would prefer to have, their answers tend to be remarkably similar. Typically, the description goes like this:

- Tolerance consistently prevails throughout the organization.
- People are energized, cheerful, flexible, positive, and knowledgeable.
- The work is balanced between the challenging and the tedious.
- Work is shared.
- Everyone shares ideas.
- People are willing to be team players.
- Everyone enjoys his or her job.
- Change is embraced.
- People are focused on the same whole vision.
- They are happy to come to work.

When I ask the same people if they think the workplace environment they described is actually possible, the response is mixed. A few believe it is possible; others believe just as strongly that it is not. Most are somewhere in between. Typically, some will say, "It depends on the library director."

Is this ideal kind of workplace possible? Yes, it is. The director plays an important role in providing the leadership for it. However, the workplace we say we want depends on what happens, day in and day out, at the individual level. Every person in the organization is either making the workplace better or making it worse. There is no neutral ground. Each decision, action, and behavior makes the organization either more effective or less so. The following example illustrates this. It occurred in an organization whose situation had so deteriorated that one individual was on the verge of suing the employer.

Tom claimed that management did nothing to correct the hostile work environment in his work unit. In fact, management had failed to see the seriousness of the situation and to take corrective measures. This lack of action made the situation worse.

Still, the initial hostility was not between employees and management. It was the result of behavior exhibited by individuals in the work unit toward one another. In this case, it was rooted in one person's intolerance of another's sexual orientation. The hostility began with two people and eventually spread to everyone in the unit. People on the fringes of the dispute eventually took sides. There was no neutral ground.

The environment became the antithesis of the desired workplace. Everyone's work was negatively affected. Productivity declined; other work units were impacted. Resentment began to grow throughout the organization.

Fortunately, management finally did take action. In addition to short-term remedies, management also provided coaching for individuals in the unit, including the unit's new manager. First, the coach helped individuals work through the crisis. Then for many months the coach worked with the group and individuals in the group to help them build the skills they needed to work effectively together.

Coaching is not a solution to every situation. However, it is a tool for improving the effectiveness of individuals and of teams—and in doing so, of the organization as a whole.

WHAT IT MEANS TO COACH

Coaching is the purposeful and skillful effort by one individual to help another achieve specific performance goals. The coach facilitates the player's attainment of the player's goals. The success of this effort depends on the cooperation of both parties. The player is willing to be challenged, supported, and influenced by the coach. The coach enables this willingness throughout the stages of coaching. However, the full meaning of coaching can only be grasped by understanding its purpose, which varies from situation to situation.

Coaching is a multidimensional concept. That is, it has many possible applications on many different levels. Pretend for a moment that from a vantage point outside and above the building, you are literally looking into the library. For several

moments, you are able to observe all of the coaching as it is happening. Every coaching situation is a pulsing light. You have the ability to look in on, observe, and hear each coaching interaction. There, at the reference desk, is one between two coworkers. There's another on the loading dock. There's one moving down the hallway. Over in the office is another between an employee and her supervisor. In another office, a consultant is coaching the director. The digital-divide project team is meeting on the mezzanine, where the team leader is at the moment coaching the team. The senior leaders are in a communications work session in the basement. They've been working on improving communication throughout the organization. They are in a biweekly debriefing session with their coach from HR.

You are aware of every meeting, every gathering, every e-mail, and every phone conversation where coaching is happening. You hear parts of each coaching dialogue. You observe coaching in various forms and applications. From this vantage point, you see an organization that has internalized coaching practices and behaviors. It occurs to you that these independent interactions are part of a multidimensional learning process that is happening throughout the organization.

The meaning of coaching changes, too, depending on whether it describes an event, a style, or a strategy. Saying that a manager has a *coaching style* suggests that his dominant mode of interaction is facilitative rather than directive, for instance. *Coaching strategy,* on the other hand, refers to the approach that will be taken in coaching a particular situation. Any attempt to define coaching must acknowledge these various applications and dimensions, all with somewhat different purposes.

Tutoring, Counseling, and Mentoring

In the course of coaching individuals, the coach may tutor, mentor, and counsel individuals, too. These functions are sometimes needed to help individuals achieve their performance goals. People generally use these terms and the term *coaching* interchangeably. In this book, however, each has a different meaning.

Tutoring is a form of instruction in a particular task or for a particular occasion. For example, the coach might tutor an individual in preparing a presentation for the library board. Developing the presentation style, duration, approach, and so on are the subjects of the tutoring. Worried about doing this well, the player confides this fear to the coach. The coach learns that some of the anxiety is due to the player's lack of preparation. The player knows his subject, but he doesn't know how to present to this particular audience. The coach treats the player's anxiety by talking the player through a presentation format.

A coach may need to counsel an individual who confides in the course of a coaching interaction that he feels despondent over the loss of a loved one. *Counseling* means "to offer advice, opinion, direction, or recommendations on the basis of the consultation that occurs." This does not suggest that the workplace coach attempts to provide psychological or other counseling in the place of professional providers. However, in the course of coaching, individuals will convey to, confide in, and even ask the coach for her opinion, advice, direction, or recommendations on personal matters.

Individual workers are whole people. Their life circumstances and events have an impact on their performance. Helping performance generally means addressing the individual's well-being. The coach will become aware of such influences. She must responsibly decide the appropriate course for each unique situation.

Mentoring is guidance from someone who has gone before. For example, a mentor has firsthand knowledge and experience in a career path that the player wants to pursue. A librarian may be a mentor for someone who aspires to become a librarian, or a person who has climbed the corporate ladder may be a mentor for a middle manager. The mentor role assumes that the mentor has experience, knowledge, and contacts that can help a particular individual achieve a specific career goal.

Tutoring, counseling, and mentoring happen both inside and outside the coaching relationship. It is possible to mentor, tutor, or counsel individuals apart from the coaching process, and vice versa.

It is not always essential that the coach have expertise in the library field to coach people who work in libraries. On the other hand, in some situations it is essential. For instance, some libraries engage reference and other specialty coaches when the performance goal is specific to improving a particular skill set. Libraries also use "peer coaching" to improve reference and other specialized skills.

There are times, of course, where knowledge of the library industry or management is very helpful as a backdrop. Whether or not the coaching situation requires a particular expertise, the basic structure of coaching is essentially the same.

Much of the coaching discussed in this book has to do with helping individuals get past the barriers that impede their performance. What people typically struggle with is not their reference or specialty capability; it is a struggle with personal, interpersonal, and organizational performance barriers. Coaching is suited to providing this as nothing else can. Training, courses, conferences, and so on do not endeavor to directly improve the performance of individuals in the personal way that coaching does.

The Substance of Coaching

There is one constant in all coaching, regardless of its breadth, depth, or application. That constant is *change for the better*. Whether the application is a single coaching dialogue between an employee and a supervisor or a long-term organizational development strategy, coaching is about facilitating change for the better.

What is the substance of coaching? The following scenarios include ten coaching situations. Thematically, these coaching situations are generally related to interpersonal, performance, and process issues. All three themes can play a part, but typically one is dominant.

Scenario 1 is predominantly about interpersonal ineffectiveness. Interpersonal conflict can stall work at every level of the organization. The inability of individuals to effectively resolve normal workplace conflict and to accept individual differences is often a factor in hindering the performance of individuals and teams. The extent of the harm this causes to organizations depends on how pervasive the conflict is. Still, it keeps even very effective organizations from being as effective as they could be.

The process theme dominates scenarios 5, 8, and 10. In these situations, people are having difficulty accomplishing an assignment. These assignments all involve several individuals having to collaborate to achieve a goal. Processes can break down. Process is simply a matter of how one moves from the starting point to the destination. In the workplace, individuals vary in their ability to do this. A group of individuals attempting together to get from the starting point to the destination will invariably have different ideas about how to do it. Individuals and teams are more successful when they have a process strategy. Generally, this is the focus of coaching the individual, group, or team that becomes bogged down in the journey.

For example, in the headset situation, scenario 10, both advocates and opponents of headsets are firmly entrenched in their viewpoints. They don't know how to resolve the impasse. Some aren't even aware that they have a responsibility to do so. There is also an element of process coaching in scenario 3. Kathy may be impatient working with others. It is probably also true that she does not know how

to successfully bring the assigned people together to do the assignment.

The performance theme dominates scenarios 2, 3, 4, 6, 7, and 9. The purpose of coaching in these scenarios ranges from improving lagging performance in scenario 2 to achieving superior performance in scenario 7 to coaching someone out of the organization in scenario 4. All of the scenarios directly or indirectly involve improving overall performance of the individual or team and the organization. Coaching can be about performance or about anything that impacts performance, such as career change, development, advancement, personal crisis, or interpersonal conflict.

COACHING SCENARIO SAMPLER

Scenario 1

Some librarians complain—among themselves and to the new manager—about a librarian coworker. They say Sam has not carried his weight in the department for years. No one has spoken directly with Sam about this, however. The new manager, Maria, finds that the work group does not know how to effectively manage other routine conflicts as well. Maria knows that coaching may take a while, but the complaints have presented an opportunity for it. She will begin coaching individuals and modeling how to effectively resolve typical interpersonal conflict.

Scenario 2

Patricia files a grievance because she is assigned temporarily outside her department to a project she does not want to do. While awaiting resolution of the grievance, she reports to the reassignment. However, she is rude, uncooperative, and unproductive. The reassignment is upheld. Patricia returns to the new work site but remains uncooperative. Upon meeting with Patricia and hearing her out, the manager, Jorge, concludes that Patricia is angry about having no choice in the reassignment. At the same time, Jorge explores Patricia's interests and career goals. Jorge is able to suggest some work assignment options to match those interests and goals. He explains that the reassignment and having Patricia's full cooperation are

not negotiable. However, there is opportunity in her new assignment to do work that interests her and may advance her career goals.

Scenario 3

Kathy, a librarian, and three other librarians are to collaborate on a project. Kathy turns in the team product, but she has completed it without input or help from the others. Kathy said it was difficult to find time to meet together. She had no response from an e-mail inquiry to do the work online. Her supervisor, Nathaniel, knows that this promising young librarian aspires to advancement and leadership positions. He also believes that Kathy has leadership potential, but she is impatient working with others. Nathaniel meets with Kathy to coach her about how to engage and sustain the participation of teammates.

Scenario 4

After two years in higher-level management, Jerry is frequently absent and is having progressively more health and performance problems. Coaching to improve his performance has failed to get sustained, positive results in one crucial area: making decisions that make him unpopular with staff. Jerry admits his performance is lagging because he dislikes the adversarial role he feels is inherent in being a manager. In coaching sessions with his supervisor, Jewell, he speaks of changing careers.

At the same time, he acknowledges that he enjoys the status and salary of his position. It is increasingly clear to Jewell that Jerry is immobilized as well as unmotivated to resolve the dilemma himself. Jewell gives Jerry an ultimatum: he can consistently meet the performance standards of his current position for six months or be demoted to a more suitable position, be terminated, or resign. Jewell offers to provide a coach or a career counselor to help Jerry reach his decision within ten days.

Scenario 5

Perviz, a library services manager, assigns a research project to a team of four reference staff members. She believes that teaming up is necessary to involve the right stakeholders in the research design and process. It is also an opportunity to gauge the ability of these individuals to work collaboratively with unfamiliar coworkers from remote locations. When Perviz discovers that the project has bogged down, she meets with the team to learn why. She finds that the leader is frustrated with the unresponsiveness of the other team members and that they, in turn, are frustrated with the leader for charging ahead without them. Perviz facilitates the team members' airing of their grievances, helps them develop some ground rules for working together, and refocuses the team on its task.

Scenario 6

Latisha confides to John, her supervisor, that she is frustrated with a support department that has failed to meet her expectations even after she had provided them with written instructions and several clarifying e-mails. She is about ready to pull rank and take her grievance to the library director. John listens and troubleshoots the problem with Latisha. John's observations and musings from his own detached perspective essentially lead Latisha to question her initial assumptions about the support department's motives. From her newfound perspective, Latisha is able to see that pulling rank is not her only choice—or her best choice—in rectifying the problem. John and Latisha reason together about a different communication approach that Latisha is willing to try.

Scenario 7

In a meeting, Kenji, a new librarian, expresses his frustration at being underutilized in his department. Luisa, a manager who is present at the meeting, fears that Kenji's job satisfaction and professional development are at risk. Luisa invites Kenji to lunch to learn about his career interests. She inquires about Kenji's professional goals and his satisfaction with his job. Luisa focuses Kenji on his goals. She also explores with Kenji ways to use his disappointing experience as a newcomer to influence his colleagues to improve the experience for future newcomers.

Scenario 8

A staff committee is expected to develop recommendations regarding the library's integration of text-messaging questions from the public into the service program. They have met several times, but their discussions repeatedly are inconclusive. An interested manager attends one of the meetings and observes that two or three members of the committee dominate a discussion that is highly emotional. This takes the meeting off course. The manager concludes that the committee lacks a method for doing its work and ground rules for conducting its meetings. The manager volunteers to be a process coach, working with and advising the committee chair, in order to help the committee get its feet on the ground.

Scenario 9

The digital preservation program has stalled. The library risks losing two new staff members that Steve's supervisor hired to work alongside Steve. The supervisor investigates and learns that Steve is sabotaging the performance of the new staff. He is withholding information from them, refusing to plan with them, and then complaining about them to other staff. Steve has been the champion of the program, starting it and nurturing it into a first-class operation. He has been so successful that the program is expanding with funding he has obtained through grants and bequests. However, he feels he is losing control of the program with the addition of the new staff members. When coaching fails to influence the needed changes

(continued)

in Steve, he is disciplined. Steve requests a re-assignment. The new staff members are counseled, but they decide to leave the library.

Scenario 10
Some staff members want library users to use computer headsets in the library to help manage noise levels. Others balk, claiming that headsets are a public health risk. The im-passe has staff frustrated and at odds with one another. Neither side has data to support its position. Their manager, Kiyo, redefines the problem in writing. She lays out parameters for analyzing the feasibility of headsets from the library user's point of view. She then assigns a small staff team to conduct the analysis and to report findings and recommendations based on data.

Performance Barriers and Pathways to Excellence

The following pages make frequent reference to performance barriers and performance pathways or pathways to excellence. (See figure 1.1, "Ten Performance Factors.") Coaching helps individuals and teams surmount *performance barriers* and cultivate *pathways to excellence.*

Performance barriers are factors that negatively influence performance. Pathways to excellence or performance pathways (the terms are interchangeable) are desirable factors that positively influence performance. Figure 1.1 is not a comprehensive list of performance factors by any means. The list is observational, composed of nontechnical categories based on commonsense experience.

Performance barriers obstruct individual and team performance. Performance pathways enable individuals and teams to excel. Just as one or more of the performance factors can influence individual and team effectiveness, so can they influence the effectiveness of the whole organization.

Sometimes one or more performance factors are so pervasive as to seem characteristic of the entire organization. For instance, what appears to be a lack of commitment from staff may actually be the effect of a dominant performance barrier in the organization, as when whole organizations appear more or less driven by the notion that "more is better," barrier factor 6. At its worst, this notion overemphasizes production at the expense of process, relationships, principles, and other organizational essentials. One effect is that many people are pulled into that cycle by the centrifugal force of those who are so compelled. Another effect is that individual worth is often undermined to the detriment of morale and commitment. That which makes the organization appear productive in the short term in fact makes the organization less effective in the long term.

Who Does Coaching?

It is possible for anyone to coach if he or she has a mind to and has the basic skills, abilities, and characteristics. Conversations happen regularly in the organization about what isn't working and who did what to whom. These conversations are opportunities for making things better through coaching. This is one reason to encourage the development of coaching capability at every level of the organization.

Certainly, coaching needs to be in the tool kit of every supervisor at every level of the organization. Anyone who is doing performance evaluation should have basic coaching skills. Because people use the term casually and have different experiences of coaching, it makes sense to provide basic coaching training so there is a common coaching structure in the organization. Coaches can mentor one another as they apply and build skills.

Some external consultants specialize in coaching. It makes sense to develop our coaching expertise internally as well as to import coaches periodically. The coaching situation, how long it will take, who is available to coach in the organization, and other factors make contracting for external coaches a valuable alternative or complement to the internal work of the organization. It is a good idea to have a cadre of coaches in the wings. Therefore, building internal coaching strength and having one or more consultant coaches in whom you trust is good insurance.

When to Coach

Coaching is purposeful and its timing is important. Coaches do not simply react without thinking. They consider a situation and may check in with others before they decide to coach. Generally, coaching is planned in advance. However, there are times when a situation can't wait, such as in a

FIGURE 1.1 TEN PERFORMANCE FACTORS

PERFORMANCE BARRIERS	PATHWAYS TO EXCELLENCE
1. Weak ego Has needy ego Needs praise or credit Lets ego become overinvolved in the task or issue	**1. Strong ego** Has quiet ego, ego balance, and ego management Communicates about the right things—the work of the organization; not overly focused on self
2. Either/or thinking Is compulsive about policy enforcement Is uncomfortable with having to make judgment calls Imposes own standard of morality on others	**2. Comfortable in the gray zone** Is comfortable with ambiguity Can make necessary judgment calls Differentiates personal and organizational standards and appropriately acts on them
3. Interpersonal immaturity Believes conflict is negative Infers meaning without checking assumptions Avoids "difficult" conversations	**3. Interpersonal maturity** Believes there is life after conflict Checks out assumptions Can have a "difficult" conversation
4. Untreated fear Uses fear to rationalize or justify Resorts to reprisal Criticizes or blames Holds unexpressed expectations	**4. Treated fear** Is willing to learn Is willing to risk Is willing to question Is willing to be responsible and accountable
5. Lack of boundaries Has unrealistic expectations of others and self Feels there is no other view but own; no one else counts Does not know what the job is or isn't	**5. Appropriate boundaries** Recognizes there are other perspectives Knows that the clearer the boundaries, the better people can work Provides some structure and some form
6. Notion that more is better Feels that production is everything Perceives people as commodities Believes that no amount of effort is ever enough Gets ego rewards for suffering Works harder and still does not get things done Has an addiction to crisis	**6. Notion that better is more** Feels that product and relationships matter Considers all people in the equation Gets ego rewards for balance in work and life Works smarter, not harder Believes in sufficiency of time, people, self Knows that not everything is a crisis
7. Doing the wrong work Has underutilized talents and ability Does the work known, not the work the organization needs (operates in the safe zone) Has self-centered view of the job	**7. Doing the right work** Balances challenge and the mundane of work Challenges self to learn and grow Job viewed in context of larger organizational purpose
8. Institutional contradictions Practices expediency management Emphasizes the impression of caring Works at cross-purposes Provides short-term fixes	**8. Institutional alignment** Helps the institution become its ideal Practices authentic caring Uses practices that are purposefully aligned with principles Carefully weighs long-term benefit
9. Weak accountability Practices avoidance Lacks follow-through Lacks discipline to set or accomplish goals	**9. Strong accountability** Faces and deals with situations Provides consistent follow-through Enjoys sense of accomplishment
10. Intolerance Feels differences are bad, threatening, or to be feared Is closed-minded, authoritarian, or judgmental Feels others' perspectives are not worth hearing Is exclusive and opposes others Believes own way is the best way—even the only way	**10. Tolerance** Feels differences are interesting and has an eager curiosity about them Is open-minded and nonjudging Believes others' perspectives are worth hearing Is inclusive and integrates others Practices a live-and-let-live attitude

coaching intervention. You will see a coaching intervention in this chapter's "Application" section.

Sometimes the "coachable" moment arrives unexpectedly. There is often tacit agreement, and the coaching occurs. For example, coaching happens in a conversation or during a lunch meeting without a formal reference to the fact. Coaching involves noticing what is going on with individuals. When you do that, the present may be the time to make the coaching overture. Coaching includes deciding on a moment's notice to make an overture, even before the needs are named or formal agreements are made.

Coaching isn't the answer to every situation. An assessment of the situation helps the coach make this determination. The likely outcome may not warrant the time and effort it will take to produce results. Furthermore, coaching may not be an affordable option, or it may not be the appropriate course, because some situations need to be managed rather than coached. On the other hand, as you will see in the application at the end of this chapter, a little coaching goes a long way. There are times when the coach must quickly decide to intervene to address an immediate problem.

Some situations need to be managed before coaching can be applied. In the example in the "Prelude" section involving Tom, management had failed to see the seriousness of the interpersonal conflict in a work unit until it became a crisis. Managing the crisis so that stability could be re-established was the first priority. For the short term, managing included being directive with staff about ground rules, appointing an interim manager, and hiring a coach to help stabilize relationships so that the work of the unit could continue. Later, coaching also played a role in building the interpersonal skills of the staff members and the coaching skills of the manager.

Anyone who coaches and is also a manager typically must decide when a situation calls for coaching, when it calls for management, and whether and in what proportion and sequence it calls for both. Sometimes supervisors are inclined to coach a situation when they should be managing it or vice versa. Training and coaching for supervisors can help them become increasingly adept and efficient at making these pivotal decisions.

Coaching and management processes are not mutually exclusive. Every situation is unique and must be thoughtfully assessed. Coaching frequently has a role in making things better in the library, but it is not the only solution nor is it always the best solution.

Mindfulness and Coaching

Mindfulness is one of the distinguishing characteristics of coaches. They observe what others don't see and, in the course of coaching, draw the players' attention to those things. Mindfulness means that coaches are consciously aware of what is happening around them in the workplace; it is a requirement of coaching. Why is this important? The reality is that people in the workplace become absorbed in tasks and distracted for various reasons. They can miss the subtle and the not-so-subtle data that are right around them. This was the case, for instance, in the "Prelude" example when managers overlooked Tom's hostile work environment until he threatened to sue them.

When people are absorbed, they miss important clues and signals. Coaches must almost always be mindfully aware in the workplace. This conscious awareness alerts them to situations they can influence for the better or may give them information that will be important later, even if there isn't an immediate need to coach. It isn't as if the coach is only walking around being mindful of coaching situations. Rather, it is that the coach develops this quiet, observing capability and has it turned on in the workplace. The organizational milieu is full of information about what is going on. Coaches' observational abilities are strengthened as they condition themselves to be mindfully aware in the organization. As you will see in this chapter's application, conscious awareness can save the day.

Levels of Coaching

The levels of coaching vary from basic to complex and from short-term to long-term. The level of coaching is a decision coaches make based on their preliminary assessments of situations. In a preliminary assessment, coaches consider what needs to be accomplished in the context of applicable variables.

The coaching level assessment two-by-two is a tool for analyzing a coaching situation. Dividing a square into quadrants creates a two-by-two: two quadrants on top, two beneath. Values, such as "duration" and "depth," are assigned to the vertical and horizontal axes of the square. The coach uses this tool to structure thoughts by considering

---

FIGURE 1.2 Two-by-Two Coaching Level Considerations for Scenario 1

DURATION — Short ... Long

DEPTH — Basic ... Complex

Basic short

Basic communication skills
   training (as a group)
Individual coaching
One-to-one coaching regarding actual interactions

Basic long

Interpersonal skills acquisi-
   tion with practice
Practice, eventual behavior
   change
Modeling of coaching style
   versus critical style

Complex short

Interpersonal coaching
Coaching the history-laden
   interactions
Interventions as needed

Complex long

More than a dozen people
   involved
Varying levels of interpersonal
   competency
Lots of history together
Will need sustained
   individual and group work

---

all the quadrants when thinking about a particular situation. The coach makes note of coaching considerations pertaining to a particular situation in the applicable quadrant or quadrants.

The analysis generally shows that there are things the coach can do right away without having to take an all-or-nothing approach. Using a two-by-two helps a coach get a feel for the level of coaching the situation will require by allowing her to look at more than one factor at a time.

What may seem obvious about a coaching situation often isn't, until you do the two-by-two assessment. It is a helpful exercise, if only to validate the coach's instinctive assessment. For example, figure 1.2 shows the coaching-level considerations for scenario 1 (presented earlier in this chapter). The coach makes notes in the appropriate quadrant as she thinks through the circumstances of the situation.

Scenario 1 is a very complex situation requiring a long-term effort. Even so, there are some basic strategies the coach can pursue short term that will improve conditions in the department. There are also strategies the coach will need to continue if

individuals are to choose to behave differently with one another. The coach wants the department members to learn how to resolve normal workplace conflict. Being able to do this is the basis of a high-performance work unit. The coach's written comments in all of the four quadrants indicates that there are many considerations and possible strategies, and therefore many levels of coaching possible.

I know that coaching is needed at many levels in this department. There are more than a dozen individuals, and all are at varying levels of interpersonal ability. For some, coaching to build interpersonal skills will be basic while for others this will be more complex. People can be introduced or reacquainted with basic skills fairly quickly and easily, but real behavioral change will take time for practice, reinforcement, and repeated success.

Some possible strategies include initiating a basic communications refresher for the group, either as a whole or in smaller groups, and reinforcing the basic skills in individual and one-to-one coaching. These belong essentially in the basic and short-term quadrant.

There are three or four individuals in the department who have more interpersonal difficulty than the others. If they can improve, that would go a long way toward improving the overall effectiveness of the department. I can work with them one-on-one and also coach them as they and another member of the department practice having difficult conversations. These strategies belong in the complex, short-term quadrant.

Of course, if interpersonal relations improve in the department, it will be because people keep practicing. The whole department has gotten into the habit of finding fault with one another. Their comments to and especially about one another generally concern what someone else has done wrong and rarely what someone has done well. They give each other little positive feedback, and difficult conversations are strictly off-limits.

I must consider how far I can take all of this, and I must think this through at the start. It won't help the department if I start them on a course I cannot help them finish. Such a course will entail my modeling a coaching style rather than a critical style of interaction. I'll need to continue coaching individuals and interactions between members of the department while they gradually integrate the basic skills. These strategies belong in the basic, long-term quadrant.

There are several long-standing feuds in the department. Strategies to improve interpersonal relations between feuding individuals are generally complex and certainly can require long-term coaching. My role may be to refer one or more individuals to counseling or to recommend private coaching. The level of coaching and the amount of it that I can do in the department may be enough for the willing individual. However, the recalcitrant individual may not warrant the level of effort, compared with other strategies. Coaching interventions will undoubtedly be needed to stabilize these difficult personalities from time to time. Otherwise, it may be that these individuals will need to be managed rather than coached: with ground rules, directives, and consequences to those involved.

Using the two-by-two shows coaches that a seemingly daunting situation can be addressed in increments that gradually make things better. It helps coaches plan for resources and approaches they might not think about without this kind of analysis.

Scenario 1 considerations reveal that coaching can occur at every level. In contrast, the consider-

ations in scenario 4 result in plotting the level of coaching in the complex/urgent quadrant. (See figure 1.3.) Note that the variables along the axes are different for each scenario. The coach determines these variables.

In scenario 4, the ultimatum for a decision within a brief, fixed time period makes this an urgent situation. The high stakes for Jerry and the library also make this a complex coaching situation. Therefore, the coach has made urgency one of the variables and complexity the other in the two-by-two.

As the coach visually makes her way around the quadrants, she realizes that there is essentially nothing about this case that fits into the left (not urgent) side of the two-by-two. Therefore, she gravitates to the urgent/complex and urgent/not complex quadrants of the two-by-two and there muses about this case.

I know that Jerry's supervisor has stipulated that Jerry must make a decision about his future with the library within ten days. This makes the situation urgent.

Business as usual is not one of Jerry's options: He may not retain his current position, title, and salary without making the decision that he will perform satisfactorily in that position. If he makes that decision, he has been told he will be terminated unless he consistently performs satisfactorily for six months. His other two options are a demotion or his resignation. The substance of my coaching is limited and focused on helping Jerry make one of three decisions. However, the stakes are high for Jerry and the library, and this makes for a complex coaching situation.

My job as coach is to help Jerry think through his options, weigh them, and make a decision that is in his best interests. The decision, of course, is ultimately Jerry's. Since Jerry has been unable to commit himself to his current position or to leave it for something else of his own accord, I suspect Jerry will feel extremely pressured by the ultimatum. Jerry has admitted that his performance is unsatisfactory and acknowledges that meeting the standards of the job goes against his grain. Nevertheless, he may feel entitled to the job, and the pressure of the ultimatum may force him into a different decision: to legally challenge library management in a lawsuit. This adds to the complexity of the coaching.

Using a tool like the coaching level two-by-two helps coaches think through the work ahead. They can see options that may not initially appear obvious. They find their focus when, as in Jerry's sce-

FIGURE 1.3 Two-by-Two Coaching Level Considerations for Scenario 4

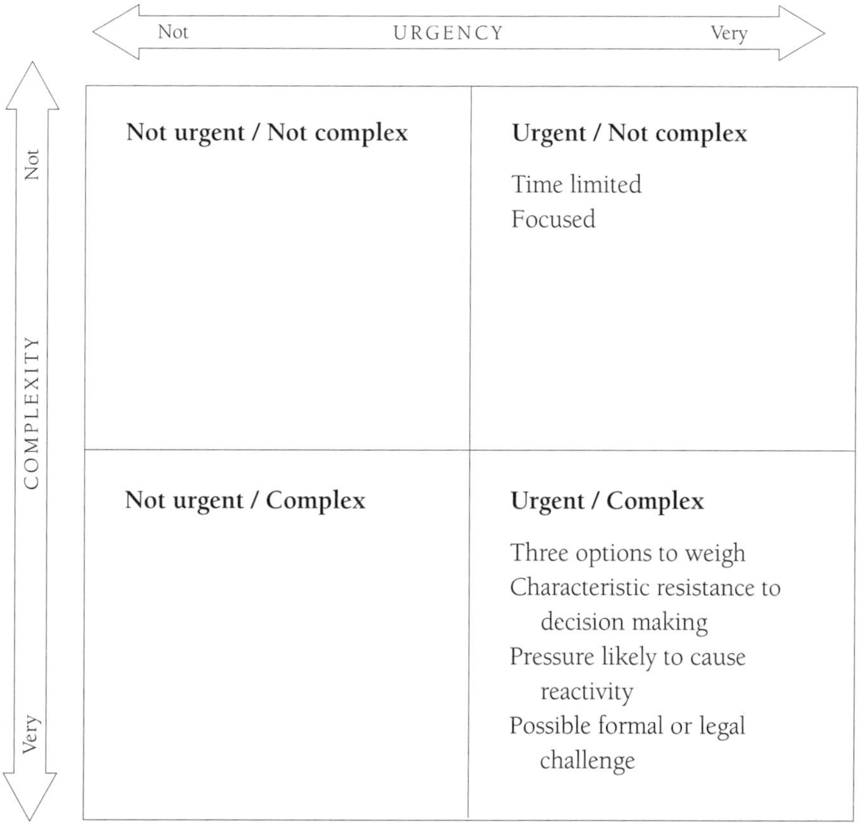

	Not urgent / Not complex	**Urgent / Not complex** Time limited Focused
	Not urgent / Complex	**Urgent / Complex** Three options to weigh Characteristic resistance to decision making Pressure likely to cause reactivity Possible formal or legal challenge

nario, the stakes are high, matters are urgent, or time is limited. This helps coaches think about their coaching strategies. It helps them weigh the likely benefits of various strategies relative to the resources it will take to treat the situations. The two-by-two also helps them assess how much time will be needed in relation to the amount of time and resources available. Coaches will want to consider how much effort over what period of time will be directed toward the player's improvement.

The coaching relationship often remains in place for a long time, even though coaching interactions have become infrequent or are not engaged in regularly. The following example shows a spontaneous coaching interaction occurring between the coach and Maya. The coaching level in this initial interaction is basic and short-term. However, it is the start of a coaching relationship that gradually involves complex, long-term goals.

Maya unexpectedly dropped into my office. She was looking for immediate feedback from me about a written job application narrative she was submitting

the next day. Time was a significant factor in determining the level of coaching I could undertake with Maya because we only had about thirty minutes.

After I read Maya's job application narrative, I focused my feedback on the most obvious impressions. The narrative was for a supervisory position in the library. Maya had written this narrative in response to a question requiring her to explain her supervisory experience. However, she had never been employed in a supervisory position. Two things were obvious from my reading: First, Maya had not made a strong case for herself in what she had written. Second, what Maya had written also sounded unsure. I said as much to Maya, and she was receptive. With a few questions, I was able to elicit Maya's supervisory experiences in and out of the library.

She told me that this discussion had helped her see the value of that experience and its applicability to the job she was seeking. At the beginning Maya said, "I hadn't seen the relevancy of that part of my past. I also had not thought through what makes a position supervisory."

I found that with coaching, Maya became more

confident about her suitability for the job. Consequently, she made changes in her application that increased her confidence and made her application more compelling.

The level of coaching is revisited along the way. Circumstances change as the coaching process evolves. Contextual factors influence the decisions about when and whether to coach. For example, in scenario 4, circumstances will change when Jerry makes a choice from among his options. Other considerations that enter into determining the level of coaching are how much the player must learn to achieve a goal, the difficulty of what the player must be able to consistently do, and the dedication of the player.

For example, Maya's immediate goal was to submit a competitive application for a supervisory job. This required basic coaching. However, suppose that Maya's long-term goal was to become a library manager. The distance Maya must go to become competitive for a management position is substantial: she has held no supervisory position at all, so she would be starting as an entry-level supervisor. She would probably spend perhaps three years learning policies and procedures, personnel administration, unit operations, and basic budgeting and planning. In this case, Maya would need to acquire the skills and abilities of a manager through supervising at various levels. She would need to prepare herself through reading and course work or classes. Maya would have a lot to learn. Under these circumstances, coaching Maya would be a long-term process.

Furthermore, coaching Maya for a managerial position would be additionally complex if she has difficulty working with and motivating others. As a supervisor, she must be consistently able to do this. Learning how to effectively motivate others to produce the work would mean that Maya would need to change some of her well-established behaviors, and this would be a long-term, complex process.

The level of coaching complexity is influenced by the dedication of the learner. Suppose Maya's main motivation to become a manager is to earn more money than she does as a librarian. How willing and able is she to do the work involved in achieving the goal? How willing and able is she to do what is difficult for her? The chances are that Maya's interest and determination would wane as she grapples with the aspects of supervision that she finds unpleasant or unnatural to her.

Coaching: A Process

Coaching is a process. As you've started to see in the two-by-two coaching level assessments, coaches facilitate a process that will result in a change for the better. Coaches help individuals or teams move from where they are to a chosen destination. The coach and the individual or team are in a coaching relationship while en route to the destination. This process generally entails more than a single coaching interaction.

Not only is coaching an overall process, but each individual coaching interaction is a process unto itself. Even in a single coaching dialogue, there is a starting point and a destination; there is a beginning and an end. Throughout the process, whether it is a single session or many sessions over a long time, the information gleaned informs the process. The coach provides specific feedback, encouragement, and an accurate reflection of progress while cultivating a relationship of trust and support with the player.

This process of coaching requires a sustained effort. Even a single coaching interaction requires some follow-up. More often, coaching is a protracted process because it takes time for people to improve and to develop. The player is headed toward a goal but frequently is on a zigzag trajectory. The coach provides feedback, and the player corrects course, gradually homing in on the goal. This is typically how people learn, and naturally setbacks along the way are to be expected.

There are two structural patterns you will repeatedly use in the process of coaching. These are the *stages of coaching* and the *coaching process framework*. These two structural patterns will serve you well: the first when you are in a coaching interaction with a player, and the second when you are mentally processing a coaching situation. The first is a pattern of interaction with the player. The second is an intellectual construct the coach uses to understand the nature of a particular coaching case. Both of these structural patterns are demonstrated in one or more of the coaching applications at the end of the chapters.

The Stages of Coaching

Coaching consists of the initial, content, and wrap-up stages. Coaches work through these sequential stages in conducting coaching interactions. Each stage has a different objective: to introduce, to get to the substance, and to bring closure. The stages of coaching can also be applied to the coaching relationship, consisting of many interactions over a period of time. Even in a long-term coaching relationship, there are initial, content, and wrap-up stages of that relationship.

The Initial Stage

During the initial stage the coaching relationship is established. The coach and the player have come together to work on something in particular. In the initial stage, that particular something is named by them, and they agree to proceed. This agreement may be easy, quick, and almost tacit. On the other hand, the initial stage of coaching can take time and considerable skill just to arrive at the coaching agreement.

For instance, a person whose performance is lacking may be reluctant to be coached. Yet the person's effectiveness, advancement, and even her continued employment might depend on being open to coaching. Skilled coaching actually begins in the initial stage, when the coach must help the reluctant player see how it is in the player's interest to accept coaching.

The initial stage of coaching is the presenting stage. The issue is put on the table by either the coach or the player, and the coach and player agree to have a substantive dialogue. For example, in scenario 6:

> Latisha initiated the coaching session with John and presented her frustration with a support department. Her frustration with the support department was the presenting issue.

Gaining the player's agreement is dependent on the player's ability to trust the coach. Sometimes trust is already established at the point of presentation. At other times enough trust must be established in short order for things to move forward. It is crucial to establish enough trust that the player agrees to proceed.

The Content Stage

The content stage of coaching centers on understanding the real nature of the presented issue. It is in the content stage that the coach and player examine and develop their understanding of the issue. This is achieved through dialogue that leads to clarity and understanding. The coach and player home in on the issue.

> With Latisha, John listened and was sympathetic, and then gradually shifted into an examination of what was at the heart of Latisha's frustration. (This shift was the beginning of the content stage.) With a few thoughtful questions, John helped Latisha discover that her frustration came from having received a product from the department that failed to reflect her careful instructions. Latisha felt she had done her best to communicate what she wanted, yet the product was far off the mark. She had begun to think that the departmental representatives she had worked with were discounting her. She was ready to go over someone's head now to get satisfactory work.
>
> John helped Latisha reason with herself about what to make of the department's unsatisfactory response. Was it personal? Was Latisha being intentionally discounted? Was this caliber of work typical in her experience of this department? What else might be going on so that the work missed the mark?

The content stage also explores options and possible courses of action the player might take to address the real issue.

The Wrap-up Stage

The wrap-up stage of coaching brings closure to the session or, when the coaching has entailed multiple episodes, to the process. There is a resolution about what will be done as the result of understanding gained in the coaching session.

> Latisha's realization that this caliber of work was atypical led her to conclude that the department was probably swamped with work and not following instructions as well as usual. Latisha decided that she would personally speak to the department manager and ask for his help in getting the product redone to specifications.

In this stage, the coach summarizes the issue and any agreements about next steps. The coach acknowledges the player's effort and validates the work that has been done by the player. The coach encourages the player, projecting confidence in the player's ability to accomplish what is ahead.

Although the stages of coaching are essentially the same for every coaching situation, the amount of coaching needed in each situation varies in complexity and duration. The strategy is relatively simple in the coaching interaction with Latisha. All three stages were completed in a twenty-minute coaching dialogue. What the scenario did not say was that this was one dialogue in a long-term coaching process in which the coach and Latisha were working together to cultivate a stronger ego in Latisha. A stronger ego would help her more easily get the response she needs from others and effectively communicate her workplace needs. This, in turn, would help her accomplish her performance goals.

No matter how compelling a case the coach makes, coaching cannot be effective without the true cooperation of the player. Coaching cannot be forced. It is the player who actually does the work, makes the improvements, and changes behavior. The coach helps from the sidelines by giving feedback to the player, naming the player's accomplishments, and noting when the player is backsliding. The coach provides encouragement and an accurate reflection of progress.

Coaching Process Framework

The coaching process framework is a structure for coaches to use as they think through coaching situations. It has four elements:

- observation
- diagnosis
- prognosis
- treatment

Within this framework, the coach intellectually processes the situation while moving from problem to solution. This mental processing gets the coach to the crux of the matter.

Observation means coaches take in data and information, initially and throughout the process. Coaches also diagnose the condition; that is, they identify the condition from the signs and symptoms they observed. Essentially, the diagnosis is a decision the coach reaches based on observation and analysis of information. It is a conclusion about the nature of the problem.

The prognosis is a reasoned, experienced speculation about the outcome of the present situation given various alternative courses. It involves looking at and weighing options for treating the condition. Coaches ask, "What is the probability that this condition can be successfully treated? What will it take?"

Treatment is the chosen remedy for the condition—the action element of coaching. It is what will be done to treat the condition. Treatment includes follow-up by coaches to monitor the progress and the condition of the player.

Coaching Affects Consequences

The wonderful thing about coaching is that when things go wrong, coaching can help make the best of it. We are imperfect, and we live in an imperfect world. Things don't always go as planned, mistakes happen, events occur, and people react unpredictably. When things go wrong, we have a tendency to panic, to blame, and to react. Under these conditions, reality may be distorted, for it is viewed through the filter of our experiences.

As a detached observer, the coach can help assess the true damage and provide feedback. Since the coach is also mindful about organizational effectiveness, he brings a perspective to the situation that is apt to be broader than that of the person who is in the middle of a controversy.

As shown in scenario 6, even minor occurrences between individuals have consequences for organizational effectiveness:

> John, the coach, listens, reflects, and asks clarifying questions. He poses questions and does not try to solve the problem. The questions are those that occur to him as Latisha's story unfolds. They are the right questions because they have come out of his intent to understand. From a detached perspective, what John makes of the situation after hearing the story is that staff of the offending department are probably not willfully defying or slighting Latisha. Latisha is just not getting through to them.
>
> "After all," Latisha says, "this is certainly uncharacteristic of the department's past performance."
>
> John listens and reflects. Then Latisha comes up with a different approach to communicate what she needs. Her approach gets her the results she wants.

What the coach did, though seemingly innocuous and simple, enabled Latisha to work through her frustration before taking it to the offending department or to the director. John listened attentively, posed insightful questions, made thoughtful observations, and gave honest feedback. John allowed himself to be a sounding board for Latisha, who then discovered her own solution.

Short-Term versus Long-Term Results

Coaching is a tool for producing both short-term and long-term results. For example:

> Ellen, a prized employee, suddenly announces to her manager that she is leaving library employment. In the short term, the coach, Darla, persuades Ellen to defer her decision.
>
> In the coaching session, Darla learns that Ellen feels completely overwhelmed by her work. The coach is able to listen and to acknowledge Ellen. In the ensuing dialogue, the session results in a temporary workload relief plan that satisfies Ellen. Ellen also observes how Darla works with her to reset priorities, defer projects, and provide her with additional help. Darla assures Ellen that finding a long-term solution is of the utmost importance and outlines on a sheet of paper the next steps, according to their agreement. This outline includes a schedule of regular meetings to check on the success of the temporary work plan and to provide an opportunity for Darla to assess and coach, as appropriate.

Of course, this is a short-term remedy. The employee has signaled extreme distress, seemingly without warning—a sign that all is not well. Is something going on with the employee, the workload, the manager, communication between them, all of these, and maybe more?

> The manager knows that she must begin a process of fact-finding to diagnose the situation. The meetings she and Ellen have agreed to will help diagnose the problem.
>
> The long-term result may be that Ellen leaves the organization. It may be that some work process improvements take place or that the manager learns that she must check in more frequently with some employees than others. Ellen may learn that she can ask for help much sooner or that workload realignment is permissible.

Coaching Terms, Techniques, and Tools

The relational map of coaching terms (figure 1.4) is a guide to the terminology frequently used in *Coaching in the Library*. These terms are all elements of an organic, not mechanical, coaching structure. The map shows the categories of terms you have already encountered (the definitions, levels, stages, process framework, attributes, and tools) or will encounter later in this book. The following sections of this chapter build on this lexicon by explaining the types of coaching relationships and techniques.

Coaching Relationships

Terms like *coaching situation, coaching interaction, coaching meeting,* and *coaching dialogue* provide a common vocabulary for talking about the coaching relationship. A *coaching situation* is the context in which coaching occurs. The scenarios, examples, and applications in this book are all coaching situations that practically or potentially involve a coaching relationship. A coaching situation may require several or many coaching interactions, meetings, and dialogues.

A *coaching interaction* occurs between the coach and the player or players. This interaction may happen in a face-to-face meeting, over the telephone, in an e-mail exchange, and so on. It is an interaction in which both parties are purposefully addressing the player's performance or related issues. The interaction includes a *coaching dialogue.* This is the give-and-take conversation that occurs between coach and the player.

A *coaching meeting* may or may not be a formal, prearranged one. It may be a chance meeting in the hallway, a telephone session, or a coaching interaction that unexpectedly comes about during a casual lunch. It includes an interaction in which both parties are purposefully addressing the player's performance or related issues.

Coaching Techniques

Confronting, giving feedback, the coaching intervention, and process coaching are coaching techniques that frequently come into play. All are described in greater detail later in the book and are demonstrated in examples and applications.

Confronting means that the coach skillfully draws the player's attention to a performance-related behavior, occurrence, or condition for which the player is responsible. Here's a simple example. Monica, an employee of the library, dropped off some supplies at one of the library facilities. Monica parked in the loading zone near the employee entrance. As she prepared to unload the supplies from her car, she realized she did not have her key to enter the building. Fortunately, a shift was ending and an employee was exiting the building

FIGURE 1.4 Relational Map of Coaching Terms

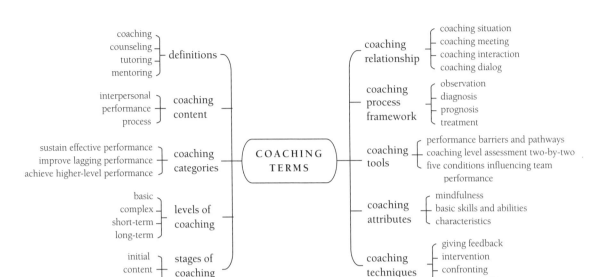

just as the box-laden Monica was approaching the door. Monica asked one, and then another fellow employee to hold the door open for her while she unloaded a couple of boxes from her car. The first employee said she couldn't because she was on her way home. The second deliberated for the twenty seconds it would have taken him to oblige Monica, then acquiesced.

What the coach does with an incident like this is to follow up with Monica and her fellow employees. In this case, it was possible to identify the second employee, Jim. The point of following up with Monica is to understand what occurred, to attend to Monica, and to coach her, too. Why coach Monica? Monica was reluctant to tell anyone in authority about the incident. She didn't want to get anyone in trouble. However, Monica had told a coworker, and the story was making the rounds. Understandably, Monica was focused on how this incident affected her. But Jim's behavior might be typical of how he treats other employees and library users. Monica needs to know that bringing the incident to someone's attention was the right thing to do. She also needs to know that the consequences for the customer must always be considered. Finally, she needs to know that "getting Jim in trouble" is not the inevitable consequence of her reporting the incident to a supervisor.

The point of following up with Jim is to influence how he handles future situations of this

kind. Jim explained that he deliberated because he was absorbed in his work. He was just trying to do his job. The coach, his supervisor in this case, explained that there is more to doing the job than just doing the work. Doing the job means taking the time to help a fellow employee. The coach wanted Jim to consider in the future the possible consequences of his actions. How had Monica felt? How might a customer or library board member feel if he had been the one asking for Jim's help? The coaching dialogue clarified expectations and priorities for Jim.

By coaching Monica and Jim, the supervisor made things better with Monica and Jim. Now Jim had some guidelines for handling similar occurrences. He admitted he hadn't thought about any of those consequences, and he certainly hadn't meant to offend Monica. He really hadn't been thinking. That, he now realized, was the problem. The job includes being mindful and thinking about the consequences of one's actions.

Ordinarily, what might have happened with regard to this incident? There might not have been follow-up with Monica or Jim. The follow-up with Monica might have addressed only the facts; there might have been no attention to her emotional state. There might have been no coaching of Monica, and there might have been no follow-up with Jim. After all, it took time for the coach to follow up to the extent that she did. The interaction with Jim might have been critical rather than constructive; Jim's supervisor might have been directive or blaming. There might have been no dialogue between the supervisor and Jim to verify the incident. There might have been no coaching Jim about expectations and consequences. The supervisor might simply have assumed that there was no excuse, no circumstance that might explain Jim's behavior. She might have dashed off an e-mail admonishing him for what he had reportedly done. None of this would have made things better.

As it happened, the coach was also a bridge. Monica learned that people care about how she is treated at the library. Jim learned that people care about his behavior, too. He learned that there are consequences to ordinary decisions. He learned that people matter in this library. Jim learned that his behavior had been inappropriate and why. He learned a lesson in balancing priorities. He learned that there was more to doing the job than just doing the work. By coaching Monica and Jim, the coach not only changed for the better the consequences of this particular incident; she also reinforced the importance of treating internal and external customers with respect, a basic tenet of this library.

No matter who you are in the organization, you are either making the library better or you are making it worse. When you coach well you are making it better. Coaching and a coaching attitude help create a humane organization. Coaching helps individuals, teams, and the entire institution balance themselves amidst constant change. It does this by improving the quality and consistency of interaction in the workplace. It is, after all, our consistency of interaction, rather than the codification of rules, policies, and procedures, that leads to predictability and stability. Coaching strengthens individual and organizational durability. It poises individuals and teams in an otherwise unpredictable environment. This is the ultimate position from which to be consistently effective.

Giving feedback is a staple of coaching, and the way the coach does this is crucial to successful coaching. *Feedback* is a return of information from the coach to the player about the player's behavior, action, or other aspect of performance. For example, the coach was giving Jim feedback when she told him that Monica had not known what to make of Jim's hesitation to help her. Jim otherwise had given no thought to following up with Monica. Given this feedback, Jim realized that he should

have a conversation with Monica to clear this up.

A *coaching intervention* occurs when the coach intercedes on behalf of the player to influence a particular course of events. The decision to do a coaching intervention is often spontaneous. For example, in scenario 7 Luisa, the manager, initiated a coaching intervention. She saw that Kenji was discouraged and might be considering leaving the library. Luisa took time to encourage Kenji. A coaching intervention is generally precipitated by a coach's observation of something that needs immediate attention, such as that shown in the application at the end of this chapter.

Process coaching is a technique coaches use to help players troubleshoot workplace processes that bog down. Frequently, the technique is applicable in team coaching situations, but it is not limited to them. There is an application of process coaching in chapter 6. Several managers are being coached as they manage a hiring process. The coaching is not confined to process alone, but it includes coaching the managers individually and as a team when they encounter difficulties along the way.

WHY COACH?

Coaching makes things better in the workplace. It develops a humane organization and improves individual and organizational durability. In coaching, you are helping others help themselves and are making conditions better in the library. Likewise, if you are not helping people help themselves, you are making conditions worse. No matter who you are, no matter what your job or role, you are either making the workplace better or you are making the workplace worse. There is no neutral ground.

Coaching and a coaching attitude help create a humane organization. This is positive for the people who work there. A coaching organization—as opposed to a blaming organization—is a humane and effective alternative to the norm. It is also good for recruitment. A humane workplace is an employment incentive for most people. A coaching organization sends the message to the workforce that individual development is a high priority.

Individuals and teams need a consistent, durable place to stand in a changing and challenging workplace. Coaching helps individuals and teams balance themselves in a constantly changing and unpredictable workplace. Like the martial artist in the ready position, individuals or teams who are coached are poised for any eventuality. This is the ultimate position from which to be consistently effective.

Coaching is a tool for creating this durability. It is a reservoir that nourishes workplace resiliency and the ability to yield and rebound. It creates an environment that supports the new work and the constant learning in our library organizations.

HOW TO COACH

There is a basic structural pattern for mentally processing a situation: the coaching process framework of observation, diagnosis, prognosis, and treatment. Whether the coaching situation occurs on the spur of the moment or is planned in advance, this basic framework reliably supports effective coaching.

The following application illustrates the basic coaching framework in a coaching intervention. A manager decides in a matter of moments to do a coaching intervention with a distraught employee. Note that throughout the process, the coach is attending to the person he is coaching.

APPLICATION

THE MINDFUL COACH APPLIES THE BASIC COACHING FRAMEWORK IN A COACHING INTERVENTION

Observation

Naturally, people have difficulty at times in the workplace. These difficulties have an impact on their performance. Mindfulness allows the coach to notice these difficulties, often before others are consciously aware of them. Thus, situations can be addressed before they worsen. The following is how the coach recounted the story:

> It was mindfulness one afternoon that alerted me that Rebecca was distraught. I was walking down a hallway when I overheard her interaction with a coworker. Later, I realized I was picking up on what was an unusual reaction. It registered in my awareness. I instinctively veered off course and toward her. I asked Rebecca if everything was all right. She responded defensively and sarcastically. The tenor of her response confirmed that something was not right.

By being mindful in the workplace the coach was aware of and observed what was going on around him. He paid attention to what he observed. He inquired about his observations to verify his perceptions. He avoided making assumptions and didn't immediately react, letting the data inform him about what was happening with Rebecca as he walked by her work area.

I was on my way to a meeting and at a loss as to what to say at the moment. I paused briefly to visually observe her in a brief couple of moments, at the same time establishing soft eye contact, a natural expression of concern, while taking in her body language. "Okay," I said, though not convinced, then continued on my way. In a few seconds, I circled back to Rebecca and asked her to come with me. I led the way without knowing if she would follow or exactly what I would say or do if she did. She followed me. I found a nearby office that happened to be vacant at the moment. On the way and for the first few interminable seconds in the office, I hurriedly scanned my thoughts for how to begin this encounter. I knew a lot depended on my first words.

Based on the coach's instincts, he decided to follow up and analyze what he observed. Notice that the coach took the interaction out of Rebecca's work area to a private area. He had to think on his feet as he and Rebecca made their way to an empty office. He knew that what he would say first to Rebecca was crucial because she was defensive. He wanted her to trust him enough to stay. Fortunately, she had followed the coach, and this gave him a chance to further assess the situation. Rebecca's reaction to his first inquiry will let him know if he will have to take a different approach with her. This will be the basis for determining a course of action.

> My purpose is to make things better, not worse. My first words must convey this to Rebecca. I took a deep breath and began to speak. I explained, "When I asked a few minutes before if everything was OK, I really meant were *you* OK. You seemed distressed, and I was concerned. That's why I stopped to ask. I still am concerned. Is there anything I can do to help?"
>
> I could see Rebecca relax her defensive posture somewhat. She took a deep breath and began to speak. She spoke slowly at first; then her pace picked up as one worry after another spilled out. She spoke for many minutes. I listened without saying a word. It wasn't the time to ask a single question. I listened attentively. I was momentarily distracted by my own anxiety. The manager part of my mind wanted to know more about some of these worries so that I could fix them. However, I quickly reminded myself that now was not the time to do anything but listen. If I wanted to understand, I must bring my full attention to listening.
>
> Minutes later, Rebecca's pace began to slow. Her body posture, her facial expression, and her voice softened. She paused, and I waited. When she next spoke, she thanked me for taking the time to care. I told her she was welcome.

Diagnosis

> I realized from all she had said that I could not help Rebecca resolve any of her worries. I also knew that her level of anxiety was very high, alarmingly so for her to simply return to her work. That was the immediate issue. Rebecca was not in any condition to return to work. The longer-term issue was whether or not Rebecca was getting the professional help she obviously needed.
>
> I told Rebecca that I thought she was not in condition to return to work. She nodded her agreement. I asked her if she had sought help for all that she was dealing with. She acknowledged that these worries were big and little,

short-term and long-term. She said she had been feeling depressed and sometimes just the opposite. She had been to the doctor on the advice of a friend because she was worried about herself.

Notice that the coach sized up the situation by integrating what he observed and the additional information he got from Rebecca. The coach determined that Rebecca's problem was not something he could coach her about because she needed more help than he could provide. He also defined a related issue: that Rebecca was not fit to return to work.

Prognosis

The coach defined the problem and then he considered what to do. He thought about the consequences of next steps and weighed the level of effort he should put into the situation. He considered the available resources. He took various factors into consideration, including his circumstances, and homed in on the best course of action under the circumstances. He wanted the best, most appropriate course of action—the path that addresses the problem. Of the possibilities, what could be done to help the situation within the time available? What were the most important things to do, and in what order?

> I thought of going to the personnel department, but Rebecca might have already been there. I considered whether Rebecca's supervisor or I could help her. Then I realized that this situation needed to be handed over to a skilled counseling professional. I asked Rebecca if she was being counseled. She said she had called personnel just moments before I came along but only got through to voice mail. That frustrated her and she didn't leave a message. It suggested, however, that she was probably willing to go to counseling if I helped her connect with a counselor.

Treatment

> I knew that making it possible for her to see someone immediately was something I could facilitate. It should be a skilled counselor and someone who would make Rebecca a priority.

(continued)

I told Rebecca, "I think you should talk with either Marcus or Lynn in personnel as soon as we conclude our meeting. Would you be willing to do that if either of them is available?"

She said she would like to do that. I then suggested that I use the phone in the room to call, and she agreed.

The coach decided on a treatment plan and clearly communicated that plan to Rebecca. He felt he needed to lay the groundwork to help Rebecca connect with a counselor. Having decided Rebecca was not in condition to return to work, he wanted to do what he could to ensure that she received timely attention. Notice that during the coaching interaction, he monitored and appraised Rebecca's willingness to accept counseling at this time and in this manner. The coach was more assertive in this situation because of Rebecca's condition. However, accepting the coach's suggestion must be Rebecca's decision.

I thought Rebecca would go to personnel, but I wasn't sure the individuals I named would be there. Even if they were, Rebecca was much calmer now than she was in the hall. She had alerted me to her mood swings and her impatience (she'd not left a message when she got voice mail). Perhaps she would become impatient again or understate the urgency of her need to the personnel office attendant. If so, the counselors might not see her right away. It might be days before Rebecca connected with one of them. I decided to make a call to line up one of these counselors if possible.

When I got voice mail in the personnel office, I called the receptionist in an office adjacent to personnel. I asked the receptionist to search out either of the two counselors right away and to call me back within fifteen minutes to tell me whether he had located them.

Meanwhile, Rebecca and I talked about possible next steps. Thankfully, the receptionist called within minutes to say that Lynn had just returned to her office and was holding on the line. I then spoke with Lynn and asked if she would be able to see Rebecca within the next hour. She assured me that she could see Rebecca immediately and would await her arrival.

Again, the coach persisted in trying to facilitate the appropriate connection in personnel. He anticipated that Rebecca, in her distracted state, might not be a strong advocate for herself if she encountered even a slight obstacle. Being told to come back, call for an appointment, or wait more than a few minutes might trigger a reaction like the one in the hallway or cause Rebecca to leave abruptly. In a coaching intervention such as this, the coach is not necessarily the person who will continue the coaching that might ensue.

My immediate prescription was a referral to a trained professional counselor. I was not the best person to help Rebecca from this point on. However, my intervention was crucial to redirecting Rebecca to a course of action that was helpful to her and beneficial to the library.

Follow-up

I immediately followed up after Rebecca left to go to personnel by contacting and briefing her supervisor. The supervisor and I agreed to touch base the next day to compare notes on Rebecca's condition. I asked him to make a point of checking in with Rebecca over the course of the next few days to gauge if all was well.

Later that afternoon I stopped by personnel and visited with Lynn. I wanted to know the counselor's impressions and compare them with my own. The counselor wanted to know what I initially observed and what Rebecca had said, and I wanted to know in general how Rebecca had responded in their meeting.

The coach's mindfulness played a critical role in this case. If it were not for the mindfulness and responsiveness of the coach, Rebecca's distress could have led to a crisis for Rebecca, a library customer, another employee, or all of these. Even in cases for which the coach has little time to prepare, the coaching framework of observation, diagnosis, prognosis, and treatment provide a logical structure for handling unpredictable occurrences. In this case, a *little* coaching went a long way.

2 the effective coach

PRELUDE

What goes on in a coach's mind? She considers possible coaching approaches, weighing the merits of each. Is it something she should handle instantly? Should it wait? Can it wait? Are there other circumstances that should be considered in deciding how and when coaching takes place?

She thinks through the coaching meeting, mentally clarifying the desired outcome of the meeting. If she doesn't get that outcome at the meeting, what will she do? She considers how the player might react and anticipates questions and behaviors that are likely to surface. She mentally prepares herself for handling those should they arise.

As she begins coaching, the coach is focused on the player. She assesses what the data she is taking in means to the coaching interaction. She allows that data to inform her about what she should do now in the coaching interaction. She continuously assesses the condition of the player. She continuously takes stock of her plan, approach, and effectiveness.

The coach is mindfully engaged during and after the coaching session because every aspect and stage of coaching demands assessment and decisions. She makes decisions constantly as she takes in data from what she hears and observes, whether engaged in a session or not. She seeks out data from the person being coached and from appropriate sources to help gauge progress. She carries the situations she is coaching with her, incubating the development of strategies that will help the player.

WHAT IT MEANS TO BE AN EFFECTIVE COACH

Anyone who has the desire can learn to coach. The basic coaching tool kit contains a set of skills that the coach gradually learns to use more and more effectively. You may be reading this book to help you coach an employee whose performance is lagging, or you may be one of those people who by nature is interested in developing the potential

21

of others. Whatever your reason, once you decide you want to work on your coaching ability, you will gradually become more aware of coaching around you and opportunities for coaching in your work, home, and leisure.

The best way to become a coach is to practice coaching. The workplace is full of coaching opportunities. However, you can practice just about anywhere there are people. You will learn how to coach from the experience of coaching others, being coached, and watching others coach. The next time you are on the verge of giving advice to a family member, try coaching instead. A coaching attitude will relieve you and those you might otherwise "advise" of the burden of expectation. You are not expected to solve their problem; they are not expected to satisfy you. That is the essence of coaching. This opens people up to finding the solutions they are fully capable of finding, with a little help from a coach.

The next time you sit through one of your children's practice sessions or one of your own, notice what the coach does that is effective. What doesn't seem to work? What might be more effective? Does the coach's style vary from person to person, or is it one-style-fits-all? What is the effect? What would make it more effective? How would you do it differently? How would you improve on what the coach did?

Coaching is a purposeful approach to building worker ability and effectiveness. The coach does this by objectively observing and assessing the other's ability and performance. She provides constructive, specific feedback and offers advice or instruction on conditioning, technique, strategy, and artfulness. The coach gives feedback, advice, and instruction at the time and in a manner that optimizes the other's learning. The coach encourages, motivates, and inspires the player to persevere through the highs and lows of the player's development.

Basic Skills and Abilities

The following sections describe the basic skills and abilities the coach needs. They are easily learned. The more you practice, the more skilled you become. There are many other useful descriptions of coaching attributes in various books that I have cited in the "Selected Resources" section of this book.

Being Purposeful

Coaching is purposeful. The coach is in charge of guiding the process so that it remains purposeful. The coach brings form to the function of coaching; that is, the coach assesses the situation, determines an appropriate level of coaching, and plans for the coaching by understanding and effectively applying the observation, diagnosis, prognosis, and treatment process through the initial, content, and wrap-up stages of the coaching interaction. There is order to the planned progression of the player, and the coach guides the process through this ordered progression.

Purposefulness involves assessing a potential coaching situation on paper first and planning for the coaching interaction before launching into it. It also involves mindfully tracking the progress of the player and evaluating how the coaching process is going. Coaching equals time equals money. The cycle of planning and assessing ahead of time will help ensure that the investment of time is worthwhile all around. The coach owes it to the player, the organization, and himself to be purposeful.

Attending to the Player

Attending to the player means that the coach brings his whole attention to the player. He listens with the intent to perceive and understand the player. He is interactive and responsive. In word and action, the coach lets the player know she is being heard. The coach pays attention to the emotional state of the player through observation and inquiry. If he perceives the player is emotionally upset, he checks out this perception with the player.

The coach notices, for example, if the player appears happy, anxious, withdrawn, angry, calm, distracted, numb, and so on. He notices if what the player says about how she is doing in the coaching interaction meshes with how the player appears, physically, to be experiencing the coaching interaction. The coach respectfully deals with the immediacy of emotions and conveys to the player and reinforces through his actions that he is in this to be of help to the player.

The coach is receptive to feedback from the player. Feedback is not always verbal. Silence, posture, and facial expressions feed back the condition of the person and the status of the coaching interaction. These often convey more than words. The coach observes, notices, checks, and lets these clues inform his coaching.

Being Detached

Detachment is a state of mind that the coach brings to a coaching situation. It is a mental separation that the coach purposely makes by putting aside opinions, judgments, and emotions to objectively consider and analyze the situation and the object of the situation. Being detached means the coach remains nonpartisan, emotionally unbiased, and neutral in her feelings about the situation and the player. She does not take sides. She lets go of preconceived notions about the person or situation.

The coach's detachment enables her to sustain her objectivity. This allows her to hear, and it allows the player to speak. The instant the coach exhibits partiality or self-interest, she casts doubt on her objectivity and undermines the trust of the player. If partiality or self-interest become active in the coach, she becomes attached to the situation and ceases to listen and to observe with the learner's mind.

Listening to Understand

Listening to understand means that the coach is completely open to hearing and observing. When he does not follow something or is unsure of what he hears, he says he does not understand or paraphrases what he thinks he heard and asks for feedback from the player. For instance, the coach says, "Let me repeat what I heard, then tell me if this is correct. Okay?" This is an example of active listening.

Listening effectively is the key to understanding. The coach is listening to what is said and to what is unsaid. He is listening with ears and eyes and senses. In the listening, he is committed to understanding the player and the situation.

Being Observant and Discerning

With the player's permission, the coach sifts through a situation that the player presents in search of the object that bears examination. The player allows the coach to hold the object up to the light and slowly turn it this way and that. Both the coach and player are fixed on the object. The coach observes and reflects what she sees back to the player. The object is neither right nor wrong. The observations of the coach, therefore, are descriptive rather than evaluative. She engages the player in an undefended examination of the object. The player views the object perhaps for the first time or from an entirely different perspective.

Being Open-Minded and Nonjudging

Being open to the player means that the coach is completely able to hear what the player has to say without passing judgment. The coach cannot help the player otherwise. The objective of coaching is to help the player help himself by getting to the heart of the situation. If the player is busy defending himself, he will not be able to focus on what he must do to help himself.

If the player is able to trust that the coach is an ally and not a judge, the player can relax his defenses and open himself to seeing what he has not been able to see before. It is not only that the coach does not judge but that she also demonstrates that she is open and nonjudging. Assessing the situation—something the coach will eventually do and then redo as she gradually processes and integrates the information she takes in—is altogether different from judging. If the coach were to judge the player, the situation, or anyone involved in the situation, it means she will have formed a conclusion. The coach must steer clear of authoritative conclusions and pronouncements.

Keeping the Player-Coach Privilege

The player-coach privilege means that the player is at liberty to say what she wishes about the coaching situation, interaction, or relationship. However, the coach is not at liberty to talk about it, except with the express permission of the player.

Effectively Analyzing, Reasoning, and Strategizing

Coaching entails assessing what is going on and thinking about and through possible solutions. It requires being able to imagine, explore, and quickly sift through many alternative strategies to home in on the best strategies under the circumstances. Throughout the process, the coach is called on to assess, plan, decide, and hypothesize over and over again.

Giving Feedback Effectively

The coach is able to effectively feed back information and observation to the player: "This is what I observe, and this is the effect." The feedback is limited as opposed to broadly cast over a range of issues or behaviors. Broadcast feedback (saying, for example, "You always do a good job" or "You are highly critical of staff") is not useful to people. Useful feedback is specific and descriptive; it focuses on behaviors and on what the coach hears from and observes about the player. It is relevant and timely. The coach describes behaviors and conditions without ascribing meaning to them. If the player's performance is unsatisfactory, the coach is specific about what precisely is unsatisfactory and why.

Most libraries already have a feedback mechanism in place: the performance plan and review process. What better way to acknowledge an individual in the workplace than to learn what she does in her job and what about her work is important to her and to give her substantive feedback about her performance? Organizations that take feedback seriously, whatever the process used, show that they value employees. The people who work in these organizations learn that they really do matter there. Each individual's workplace talents and development interests are known. The work each does is known and acknowledged. The staff members receive feedback and guidance as needed. They understand that the work they do is meaningful and know how it fits into the organizational game plan.

The following scenario illustrates feedback in a performance review process. It shows how a process can work well and easily when done purposefully. Note how Jesse, the manager, leveraged this process for several different purposes.

> Roberta was smiling more and was friendlier and more engaged than she had been. When she'd first started her new job at the college library she had been very quiet and retiring. She had kept a low profile; after all, she was new and on probationary status. What was the impetus behind her new attitude?
>
> Roberta had recently undergone her six-month performance review. With Roberta's permission, her supervisor, Jesse, invited input from Roberta's peers. Nearly all the librarians in the department agreed to participate. Jesse synthesized and organized his observations and those of Roberta's peers, some public commendations, and the comments from three other staff with whom Roberta had worked quite a bit since starting her job. At her performance review Jesse gave Roberta a written summary of these and then talked with her about them.
>
> Roberta told Jesse that she had not had any feedback from anyone until now, and she had not known where she stood with her peers. She said it really mattered to her what her colleagues thought of her and her work. As a former public librarian, she wondered what her academic colleagues and customers thought of her abilities and performance.
>
> Jesse had made this performance review process an opportunity to get to know the participating librarians in a different way. Asking them for input about a peer changed the relationship slightly. It gave Jesse information about Roberta, of course, and Jesse learned something new about each librarian. Several were receptive to Jesse's coaching them about giving constructive feedback to Roberta in the future. He talked one peer through her assumptions about Roberta's quiet manner. He coached another into checking out a perceived interpersonal misunderstanding, and with another, he modeled constructive ways to present a suggested improvement. Jesse had modeled for them how to talk with Roberta.
>
> Jesse also provided a safe environment for Roberta and her peers, a buffer zone where both the overly blunt and the underprocessed could be aired and then refined. Jesse had been the catalyst for a performance evaluation that had the desired results, and he had done it with a staff that had not experienced consistent and meaningful feedback in years. He had provided a learning zone for everyone, including himself.
>
> Roberta's performance review contained specific feedback with examples from the input of others. Roberta said she had never had such helpful feedback. She felt supported by her colleagues, who had each given careful thought to her strengths and areas for improvement. Now she knew where she stood, what they appreciated in her, and things she needed to work on. This feedback rang true to her. No wonder she was smiling more and coming out of the shadows.

Characteristics

The preceding chapter defined coaching as a process with somewhat self-contained subprocesses. The subprocesses, like movements in a musical composition, provide an organizing structure. In coaching as in the performance of a musical composition, artistry is involved as well. Within the structure, there is considerable freedom for influencing the quality of the coaching, and this can have a profound effect on the outcome of coaching. These qualities enable the coach to artfully treat each distinct coaching situation.

Self-Trust

The coach trusts herself and the process. She knows that if she fully listens and attends to the player, she will find the important questions and the important issues. By being completely open, the coach is able to discern what questions need to be asked. She trusts that she will know what to do when the time comes and that with coaching, the player will go where he needs to go.

Faith in the Player

Underlying coaching is faith in the player. The coach knows that while she must be purposeful, she is not in charge of or responsible for the outcome of the coaching—the player is. The coach has faith that the player has the ability to succeed, though it may not be on the player's or the library's terms or timeline.

The coach doesn't tell the player what to do, because giving solutions takes away the player's power to find his own solutions. Instead, the coach opens doors through inquiry, observation, and honest, humane feedback. The coach's objectivity is invaluable to the player. In the player's quest for a solution, the coach is a guide and an ally.

Resourcefulness

The coach must make dozens of decisions about all of the considerations that arise in the coaching process. His resourcefulness influences the caliber of coaching. Resourcefulness means that the coach is able to envision options, alternatives, methods, techniques, and resources that will help the player. If a player can't make the high jump using the standard technique, the resourceful coach thinks of options—one of which will work for this particular player.

Patience

Coaching respects the learning process. The effective coach works with timing and rhythm. Timing is a consideration in every coaching interaction. When is the best time this week to have that difficult conversation? Is the player ready to take the next step in his schooling regimen? What else is going on for him right now? Would this new challenge advance the player or slow down his progress? Will it motivate or discourage him? There is a rhythm to a person's learning, and the wise coach takes that into consideration. The coach understands that she must allow for the individual's developmental rhythm.

Challenging and Supportive

The coach challenges the player to the right degree. He must guard against overchallenging the player who has not yet achieved a level of conditioning for the challenge. The player can overchallenge herself by expecting too much progress before she has undertaken the essential steps to take on the challenge. The player wants the prize but is not yet ready to compete. Her failure is nearly assured, but she cannot see this.

There are also players who underestimate their abilities. They are afraid to take the next step; they are afraid to fail. Of course the next step will have some inherent risk if it is a challenge. The coach is there to support the player's decision and to encourage and accept whatever comes of the player's best effort. The coach is focused on the long term. He encourages the player through the highs and lows of the player's gradual ascent. The coach is always mindful of balancing challenge and support in the coaching relationship. The player who understands that the coach is in her corner counts on the coach's objectivity and honesty.

Self-Appraising

The coach is always working to improve his coaching. He is forever a learner. The basic skills and the qualities of the coach can always be improved. By regularly assessing coaching dialogues, interactions, and relationships, the coach learns what is more effective. The coach learns from self-assessment. He also learns from other coaches: from observing their coaching and from talking over coaching challenges. It is essential that the coach be ever curious and inquisitive about how players learn and grow. Although coaching doesn't always result in the desired outcome, it is rarely a wasted effort for either party. There are no guarantees in coaching, but there is always something to be learned along the way. The coach who isn't evaluating his work isn't fully coaching.

The coach must be vigilant about his motives. That is, coaching must always be about the development of the player and the good of the library, not about the coach. If the coach finds it is otherwise, he refocuses on the player and the library.

Discouragement invariably visits the coach as well as the player. The coach's role is to encourage the player when the player is discouraged. When the coach is discouraged, he coaches himself. Discouragement is often brought on by expectation or by fatigue. It can be a sign that something the coach or the player is doing is not working. It is just part of the process.

Discouragement, like disappointment, anger, irritation, or any negative emotional response to a coaching situation or relationship, is something to note and assess. What is causing this response, and what needs to be done about it? In difficult coaching times, the coach can draw on his basic skills and coaching qualities for his own benefit.

Self-Accepting

The coach is only human. The skills, abilities, and characteristics of the best of coaches cannot make the player do what only the player can. The coach who becomes too invested in a particular outcome is apt to be disappointed. For instance, she may want the player to achieve a particular level of performance more than the player does. The coach may put a value on her coaching based on the player making the grade the coach thinks the player should, rather than on the progress the player makes or on the benefits to the library.

Jerry, in scenario 4 from chapter 1, did not make the grade as a higher-level manager. Despite the coaching he received from Jewell for nearly two years, Jerry simply could not reconcile his own ambivalence about being a manager at this level. Jewell might have concluded that she had failed as a coach. In fact, she did all that she could, including helping Jerry eventually come to a decision. Sometimes, not deciding is a decision: Jerry's protracted ambivalence allowed him to retain the status and salary he wanted while doing the level of work he chose. Jewell's ultimatum forced Jerry to make a decision, an outcome that would ultimately benefit the library and Jerry, regardless of his choice. Success for the coach is in knowing that she has done her very best to help the player attain his goal.

WHY BE AN EFFECTIVE COACH?

There are countless instances when we can make the workplace better for people. These basic coaching skills, abilities, and characteristics will help you be a more effective manager, supervisor, team member, coworker, and employee. From the standpoint of the customer, mastering the basics of coaching is the essential element of effective employee and customer relations. People who develop and use these basic skills improve the quality and consistency of interaction in the workplace.

The effective coach models skills and behaviors that are worthy of emulation. When you are an effective coach you are contributing to improvement and making a positive difference in how you and others perform and feel about work. People who benefit from good coaching like what it does for them. They're more likely to extend the effort for someone else as a result of what they have received.

HOW TO COACH EFFECTIVELY

Probably all supervisors have wondered at one time or another why previous supervisors have not dealt with some employee's unsatisfactory performance. Coworkers and subordinates wonder, too, why no one does anything about behavior that clearly seems so obviously ineffective to everyone else.

Of course others *have* noticed, and previous supervisors may even have tried to do something about it. Perhaps they noticed but couldn't exactly describe the performance problem. They may have talked with an employee several times about his performance but saw no improvement. Besides, supervisors have many other things to do. Anyway, would they be supported by the system if they did anything?

In this chapter's application, and continued in the chapter 3 application, the topic is coaching to improve poor performance. This is the kind of coaching scenario people ask about most often. In this first part, the coach illustrates how to effectively prepare to confront a performance problem. In the chapter 3 application, the coach will actually use a coaching technique when she confronts Stan about his performance.

This application includes the internal dialogue of the coach. The coach walks herself through the process of analyzing the data she has thus far. She also plans the meeting with Stan.

The coach processes information she has received about Stan. Note that she first organizes and analyzes the initial data—written and oral feedback she has had about Stan's performance. The coach had asked for the feedback in the form of strengths and areas needing improvement. The coach is preparing to bring the concern to Stan by organizing the data and analyzing what she has thus far.

The data—both the feedback from Stan's associates and the information that will come from the meeting between Stan and the coach—are aspects of observation. Remember that observation is the first subprocess in the basic coaching process framework. The coach is inconclusive at this point because she needs to hear from Stan.

After organizing and analyzing the data, the coach shifts to thinking about the meeting with Stan. She understands, for instance, that the way she begins the meeting is important and that what she first says is especially important. The coach wants to hold the matter up to the light and examine it with Stan. How she presents or "confronts" Stan with this information will set the stage for their dialogue. In planning for the meeting with Stan, the coach thinks through the stages of the meeting: initial, content, and wrap-up. The coaching meeting—how Stan reacts and what he has to say—will further inform the situation. In the next chapter's application, the coach will confront Stan in a coaching interaction.

APPLICATION

PREPARATION FOR COACHING TO IMPROVE PERFORMANCE

Unlike the previous situation, in which the coach had to think quickly to do an intervention, coaches generally take time to prepare for the coaching interaction. Preparation is especially important in the following situation because there appears to be a performance problem that several individuals have related to the coach. In the following sections the coach is organizing and analyzing the data she has thus far before meeting with Stan, the individual whose performance is in question.

Organizing and Analyzing Observational Data

Stan is an excellent manager in nearly every respect. However, several individuals have expressed the same concern. They say that Stan's manner of interacting with others leaves them feeling demeaned and even humiliated. I've read this in the comments of a half-dozen people who work with Stan and provided their input for his annual performance review. I have some of their comments in writing; however, others preferred simply to talk with me about this matter.

Typically, feedback is a mixture of conclusions, inferences, speculations, and descriptions. It is not the whole story, but it is the beginning of it. It is an important context for understanding a problem. It also holds important information for the remedy, too.

If there is a problem and if it is going to be remedied, I will have to be able to describe the behaviors that people are upset about to Stan. If I can't do that, I won't be able to get to first base. Understanding if Stan can understand the issue—that is the beginning of improving it.

It is part of the coach's role to really understand the problem. Otherwise, there is little chance the person being coached will be able to understand it.

In the interviews with those who wanted to meet with me, I listened attentively. I have my notes of exact phrases and key words. I asked questions when I did not understand something that was said and noted examples for clarification because they help illustrate the problem. I feel that the issue will be more credible to Stan when he is able to recognize examples, phrases, and key words. I asked what would make things better. What would improvement look like? I took notes from my conversations with Stan's associates:

Anita: "Stan treats me as if I'm stupid and incompetent."

Because I want to know about behaviors, I asked Anita to give me an example, describing what it was that Stan said or did.

Anita: "I asked Stan one day about a library policy—I can't even remember what it was about. Stan told me to look it up on the intranet.

(continued)

It was the look on his face and the tone of his voice that let me know he was disgusted with me. What he told me with his look was not to bother him. There were other people around, too. I felt humiliated."

With written comments and her notes before her, the coach began an analysis of the data provided by others. Organizing her data helps her. She begins by sifting through the written comments and her notes.

First, I'll make a list of the strengths. There's a lot of commonality in what people have said about Stan. They say Stan
- is bright, "smarter than your average bear"
- is quick
- is direct
- "excels in producing high-quality, high-quantity work"
- has "a memory like an elephant"
- knows what's going on professionally
- is "on top of his subject matter"
- is "clever with words"
- does "first-class work"
- is really "devoted to his work"

The coach uses the phrases and words of those who provided them. She also makes a list of how they have said they feel about Stan's strengths.

Next, I'll look at what they said about the suggested areas of improvement:
- "He seems to get pleasure from showing that he is smarter than everyone else."
- "He makes these belittling, sarcastic comments."
- "This is a no-win situation. He doesn't give me enough information and then is impatient with me when I come to him with questions."
- "He's demanding beyond reason."

Inferences and conclusions indicate what people are making of the behavior. The coach knows that the inferences and conclusions aren't necessarily accurate. However, they will help define the problem.

Next, I'll make a list of inferences and conclusions:
- "It's as if he thinks everyone is beneath his intelligence."
- "He thinks I'm beneath him."
- "He thinks I am stupid."
- "He thinks I am incompetent."
- "He is excessively critical."
- "He doesn't care how what he requests affects me; he just wants it done and now!"
- "He is cold and uncaring."

Obviously, these statements show that Stan's associates believe that Stan thinks poorly of them. Interestingly, they think well of Stan—except for how he treats them.

Next, I'll use my notes and list the reported effects or consequences of Stan's behaviors:
- "I don't want to volunteer for assignments; I don't want to be humiliated by his criticism in front of the group."
- "I'm both afraid not to check in with him and afraid to check in with him."
- "I am relieved when he's away for a few days; the tension builds as soon as he is back."
- "He misses opportunities to collaborate because he is so quick and expects so little from everyone else."
- "I'm afraid to go to him with questions."

Finally, I'll make a list of what success would look like from the complainants' points of view:
- "I wish I could believe that he thinks I am worth having in the department."
- "I don't expect Stan to change his aloof personality. But he is so articulate. If he cares about how I feel, he could make an effort to be less insulting and derisive."

The coach asks herself what this data tells her. She makes a few notations based on the lists she has made. These will help her as she plans her strategy for the meeting with Stan.

Clearly, Stan's colleagues think well of him. The descriptions of his strengths characterize Stan as someone who strives to excel. The list of improvements actually points to behaviors that leave his colleagues wishing he would be less critical, demanding, and belittling. They have also drawn conclusions from Stan's behavior that may or may not be accurate. These individuals say they want Stan to treat them with respect. They would like to know that he thinks well of them. It is interesting that they think well of Stan, yet they believe he looks down on them. In effect, they feel that Stan intimidates them and this, they say, puts a cap on their performance. They are afraid to work with Stan because they expect him to criticize, demean, and humiliate them.

Thinking through the Meeting with Stan

The coach asks herself what she intends to accomplish in the meeting. What needs to come from this meeting? If what needs to happen doesn't happen, what is her fallback plan? She anticipates predictable scenarios that will help her anticipate and prepare to handle difficulties with calm and poise.

I consider how to begin. What will be the first thing I say? I'll take a few moments to mentally play the meeting out.

Let's see, what is the range of reactions that might occur? How will I deal with any of them if they occur? Stan may become angry, emotionally upset, or defensive, or he may deny the problem.

Answering these questions helps the coach prepare for any eventuality and gives her several key phrases that will get the meeting back on track. It helps her to prepare for the meeting by thinking through the coaching stages: the initial stage, the content stage, and the wrap-up stage. This sequence helps the coach structure the meeting to keep it on track and to control the meeting's agenda.

Initial Stage

The coach knows that the way she begins the meeting with Stan will set the tone. In the initial stage, establishing rapport and clarity about the purpose of the meeting is very important. Defining the scope or scale of the problem is an issue.

I'll need to establish that this meeting with Stan is not about finding fault. It is about facilitating

a more effective relationship between him and those with whom he works. My goal is not to judge Stan about whatever has occurred. It is to present the issue, to get more information, and to resolve with Stan what can be done to improve the relationship.

In the initial stage, I will present the issue of concern to Stan: "Stan, this is why we are here." I will let Stan know at the outset the size of this problem. That is, it is about one aspect of his work, not all of his work.

I'll say, "Here is the data and here is how I came by it. These are the behaviors that are of concern. These are the effects of those behaviors."

Content Stage

In the content stage, the coach and player examine the issue of concern. The give-and-take of the coaching dialogue further illuminates the issue. The coach's role is to hold the issue up to the light for the coach and player to examine. The coach knows that this is Stan's first chance to hear this information and respond to it. She knows that hearing negative comments is not easy. The goals of this stage are to accurately define the problem and the causes and to look at solutions.

When I have the dialogue with Stan, I'll ask Stan what he makes of what I have said to him. What does he think is going on? What light can he shed on it? I'm not sure what Stan will say. I can well imagine that he may want to know what can be done about it. Obviously, some coaching of Stan or his colleagues or of both could be helpful. Ideally, Stan will be willing to grapple with the issue. His reaction will help me analyze the concern to accurately define the problem and the effects. The preparation I did before the meeting, in the interviews, and with the list making and analysis plays a crucial role here. My demeanor—nonthreatening, nonjudging, and inconclusive—will be another major influence on how this goes.

Wrap-up Stage

The wrap-up stage resolves what will be done next. If there is a performance problem, the treatment plan is made. In the wrap-up stage, there is ownership of the problem and mutual

(continued)

agreement about what will be done next. The coach has thought about what might be done if the concerns of Stan's colleagues are either dismissed or acknowledged. Stan may want to think about the matter further. The coach considers these possibilities and is prepared to address them.

We will agree on what more, if anything, both parties will do. If this involves a timeline, we will address dates and calendars. I'll wind down the meeting so that the departure is not abrupt but respectful and cordial.

Attending to Stan

In each stage of the meeting and throughout the meeting, I will listen and be aware. I have a destination in mind, but I must be observant of conditions along the way. There will be road signs that advise me of obstacles, of times I should slow down, and of detours ahead. The feedback I get from Stan about how he is experiencing and coping with this meeting will guide me.

There, now I have a general plan for keeping the meeting on track. I have a destination in mind. However, I know I'll be at the wheel, so I am responsible for making course corrections that will help us arrive safely at the destination.

The coach has spent about an hour preparing for the meeting with Stan. She has organized the data, done some initial analysis of it, and thought through the meeting sequence. She has prepared well and can set this matter aside for the time being, confident that when she meets with Stan, the data will speak for itself. She will trust herself, Stan, and the process to take it from there.

The coach's mind wanders for a moment to tomorrow, when she will meet with Stan. She visualizes how she will welcome him, what she will say to begin the meeting, and how she will introduce the subject of the meeting. She settles on a particular visualization that satisfies her and allows herself to set the matter aside for the day.

3 coaching individuals

PRELUDE

There is a story about a man who corrected his dog for soiling the living room carpet. Each time, the man would sternly take the dog back to the soiled spot, rub the dog's nose in it, and then toss the dog outside through an open window. This attempt to correct the dog happened for three consecutive days. When on the fourth day the man found that the dog had once again soiled the carpet, he proceeded to correct the dog in the usual manner. However, on perceiving the sternness of his approaching master, the dog ran to the soiled spot, rubbed his own nose in it, and then jumped out the open window.

Like the dog's master, we can react to behavior in the workplace in such a way that our message is lost on the people we want it to influence. We think we are teaching one thing, but the individual or individuals are learning something else. The "something else" may not be good for them, for the "teacher," or for the organization. When we react negatively to or punish behavior we do not want, we are practicing negative reinforcement. Positive reinforcement, on the other hand, teaches and rewards behavior we do want. The master of the dog in the story would be positively reinforcing the behavior he wants from his dog by taking the dog outside at the appropriate times of the day—after the dog first wakes up or plays—and rewarding it with praise upon "soiling" in the appropriate location.

As you read, the last chapter's application included an example of negative reinforcement in the workplace. Anita asked Stan a question. Because he thought she should have found the answer herself, he was very brusque. Not only didn't Anita get the answer that Stan could easily have given her, but she learned to be reticent with Stan. This is undesirable behavior because in the workplace, people must be able to approach one another with questions, suggestions, and ideas. The quality of interaction in the workplace profoundly affects how well the organization functions and delivers services to its community.

What Stan meant to convey was that he expected Anita to do her homework before coming to him with questions. However, that is not what Stan said. Similarly, as the story about the dog illustrated, the critical, punishing approach to changing behavior doesn't work. Rather than getting the desired result, negative reinforcement teaches behaviors that may be more undesirable than those that are being corrected. From an organizational standpoint, things become worse instead of getting better.

When someone fails to meet our expectations in the workplace, how we react to that disappointment teaches others what they can expect from us. We are always teaching others, whether we mean to or not. If we react in anger, scold them, and "rub their nose in it," we cannot expect their performance to improve. Instead, we can expect to confuse them, or to make them afraid to approach us for the help they need. When we respond negatively to these opportunities, we are missing the chance to improve the other person's performance.

Coaching is fundamentally a commitment to teaching and reinforcing the behavior we want in our organizations. It sends the message that continuous learning is accepted practice. Coaching models how we must be with each other if we are to achieve our best individual and organizational performance.

WHAT IT MEANS TO COACH INDIVIDUALS

Coaching an individual is like putting oil in a car. You wouldn't think of operating your car without it. If you drive around a little low on oil, you know you are pushing your luck. Lack of oil causes parts to wear out and reduces the engine's efficiency and the car's overall performance. If you drive too long with low oil, you will cause some serious damage. To get your best performance you make sure the car has the right amount of oil.

The purpose of coaching may be fairly simple and immediate. For example, it may be to clarify project priorities in an individual's ambitious project portfolio. This helps the individual get back on track. Coaching may take place in a single interaction. For instance, you may have a brief meeting to encourage a discouraged coworker. On the other hand, it may be a long-term process, as when you are developing an individual's leadership ability.

The subject of individual coaching can be any-thing that has an impact on or relates to the individual's performance. It might have to do with a personal crisis, career advancement, or a project that the employee is finding difficult. It might be about resetting priorities among competing projects or about interpersonal conflict. All of these potentially relate to individual performance.

Coaching has short-term through long-term goals. For example, a long-term goal may be to develop a promising individual into a future leader, preferably in your organization. A short-term goal may be to retain this same individual who is impatient because others fail to recognize her genius and she is torn between staying and leaving.

Coaches don't initiate every coaching situation. Individuals often initiate the coaching, perhaps by presenting a problem or query to a supervisor, coworker, or other potential coach. It may be that a new employee whose performance is perfectly fine wants to know how he can learn more about the library industry because he believes this would help him, a transplant from education, do an even better job. A reference librarian who is planning for and looking forward to her retirement may be worried about filling her time when she isn't going to work every day. Another may be struggling to reconcile his vastly different management style with that of a senior manager.

Categories of Coaching

Generally, coaching individuals has one of several, often overlapping purposes. Much of the time the purpose of coaching is to help individuals do their best, day in and day out. This category is coaching to sustain effective performance. Sometimes the purpose of coaching is to improve unsatisfactory, lagging, or poor performance. Sometimes it is to help individuals who are doing fine work achieve even higher levels of performance. Once in a while the situation involves coaching someone into a more suitable position or even out of the organization.

Coaching to Sustain Effective Performance
Coaching to sustain performance is the most needed and perhaps most underused and underrated reason to coach. As you read in a number of examples, at the cost of a little time and effort, coaches can help individuals who are doing the job do an even better job. All workers, including the most exceptional performers, have moments on the

job when they can benefit from the help of a coach. With a little help, they are able to make a situation better than they might have without coaching.

For example, in scenario 6 of chapter 1, John influenced events for the better when he helped Latisha refocus on the goal of getting a good product from a support department. This was better for the library than what might have happened. John enabled Latisha to decide not to make a little problem into a bigger problem. Pulling rank would have made a bigger problem for her, the offending department, and the library director. Imagine the time and energy that would have been wasted in that approach!

It stands to reason that all individuals need to work on their performance because performance expectations are in constant flux and new priorities outweigh other priorities. Furthermore, individuals become distracted from their goals. In addition, there are skills and abilities individuals find that they do not have or that they want to improve.

Sustaining performance is dependent on individuals knowing what is expected of them and getting regular, specific feedback. Often, supervisors take for granted that individuals know what is expected of them. The supervisor and the employee have mental maps of what is expected. However, these mental maps may be very different from each other. Setting goals together certainly helps the supervisor and employee become oriented to the same map, but even when this happens, it is important to converse at key points along the way. The map is only a map, after all. It is in crossing the territory that the employee encounters obstacles and compelling distractions. These make it easy for individuals to veer off course. Performance goals are guideposts for getting one's bearings, and feedback helps individuals stay on track in the face of many competing priorities. The feedback Jim received from his supervisor about his treatment of Monica is a case in point. Jim was overly focused on the task, and the feedback from his supervisor gave him a different understanding of "doing the job."

Performance and the Absentee Supervisor
It is amazing how often we supervisors unintentionally leave people to their own devices while we attend to other things. With all there is to do, it is possible to slip into being an absentee supervisor—one who is very busy and is very product-oriented. Because communication methods are

fast and efficient, and increasingly dependent on e-mail, the part of the supervisor's job that has to do with developing the individuals who report to him tends to get little focused attention. The absentee supervisor is too busy producing to spend time enabling others to produce.

Coaching scenario 9 in chapter 1 is an example:

Steve had blazed the trail for an innovative program in his library. He single-handedly launched the program and shaped it to his standards. He operated independently. His supervisor raved about Steve's initiative and hard work. As the demand for his program grew, his supervisor added new staff. She thought Steve would be glad. She expected Steve to work with "the team." Steve had never worked with a team. It wasn't his natural style and he didn't understand how to work in a team. Steve could blaze a trail better than most, but his performance as a team member was poor. He resented having to give up his former role. He essentially withdrew from the team and continued to operate independently. The new staff became demoralized and were ready to leave the library. The program began to unravel.

In fairness to Steve, his supervisor should have prepared Steve for his transition. When individual performance is disappointing, the supervisor must examine his role in it. Is he being an absentee supervisor? Does the individual understand what the supervisor expects? The supervisor must honestly examine whether he has fulfilled his responsibility to the individual whose performance is in question.

Sustaining effective performance requires that individuals understand what is expected of them and why. It depends on the employees learning what they need to know to accomplish their performance goals. It also depends on the employees getting specific feedback about their performance. Coaching helps the supervisor and employee develop a shared understanding about the work to be accomplished. This shared understanding is not just about the functions to be performed. It is about the purpose of those functions and how they relate to the goals of the library.

Coaching to Improve Performance
This category of coaching has to do with helping the player recognize and improve performance that is unsatisfactory, lagging, or poor. Typically, this

involves something in particular about the player's performance. For example, in the chapter 2 and 3 applications, Stan's performance is more than satisfactory except in one crucial way: his demeaning behavior stifles his subordinates.

The performance barriers described in figure 1.1 often prevent individual performance from being all that it could be. It is the coach's role to accurately define the problem. Every organization is different, as is every coaching situation, but the coach would do well to be aware of recurring themes that can point to systemic problems. Such problems will need to be addressed in the long term. Minding the recurring themes can suggest complementary steps that can be taken to address these problems on a broader basis than just an individual one.

For example, interpersonal immaturity undermines performance at every level of the library. Imagine that as a supervisor, you are frequently called into situations to referee and to determine who is right and who is not. Individuals tell you the problem, ask that you not tell who told, and want you to settle things in their favor. You run back and forth between individuals, wearing yourself out in this particular situation. This isn't coaching; it isn't even supervising. Instead, such actions enable individuals to avoid responsibility for effectively managing workplace interpersonal relationships.

A condition such as this, in a work unit or whole organization, is really an insidious performance barrier. It is about the individual, and it certainly can be coached at that level. However, if this is the norm in the unit or organization, changing the situation will require a systematic effort. For example, the coach can work with the unit over a period of time to build skills in communication and conflict resolution. These basic skills are the bedrock of workplace effectiveness.

An organization is only as durable as the relationships of the people who work in it. Consistent, effective interaction leads to predictability and stability that position the organization to handle anything that comes along.

Coaching to improve performance is a given. People aren't perfect. If we want individuals to perform better, we must tell them this in specific terms. It is not effective to blame, punish, or otherwise negatively react to performance we do not want. It is effective to describe and to positively reinforce performance we do want.

Coaching to Achieve Higher Levels of Performance
This category of coaching focuses on helping individuals achieve higher levels of performance. They are performing satisfactorily, but they could perform or wish to perform at a higher level. There is something a supervisor or coach sees that suggests this is either warranted or possible. It may be that the individual identifies a skill or ability in someone she admires and she wishes to be able to do that, too. Perhaps it is that the individual is a natural leader but does not recognize it. Maybe the individual plays it safe by staying with a known job rather than risk a more demanding job she yearns to try. Maybe the individual is ready to tackle that characteristic or behavior that keeps her from advancing to that next position she covets.

Coaching to achieve higher levels of performance is not something every employee wants, but many do. Kenji in scenario 7 of chapter 1 was underutilized in his department, and he was ready to leave the library out of frustration. The coaching intervention in this scenario can help focus Kenji on alternatives that will enable him to reach past the limits others are setting for him and thereby find greater fulfillment without leaving the library. This intervention was applied in the interests of encouraging Kenji to stretch himself in the face of a frustrating obstacle by redirecting his frustration toward improving the initiation process for new librarians. The coach helped Kenji see that obstacles can also be launching pads for higher levels of performance.

You can see how the purpose of this coaching intervention is different from that of the coaching intervention with Rebecca in the chapter 1 application. In that situation, the purpose of the intervention and coaching was to sustain Rebecca through a highly charged situation.

Many individuals need encouragement to reach higher. They have a limited view of their own potential and set their sights low. Coaching gives them specific feedback about how others perceive them in the organization. Seeing a reflection of this can encourage individuals and help them visualize and achieve a more fulfilling work life. This is good for the individual and for the library.

Some individuals are hired, they are exceptional, and they are impatient.

Brian was impatient for the organization to recognize his genius. Coaching helped him develop some patience and grace until the organization could manage a proper fit. In the meantime, this coaching gave Brian a new perspective about the library. He developed a new appreciation for an organization that developed him in this way.

Others attempt higher levels of performance and learn that the job they have isn't suitable. In a continuation of the example from scenario 4:

> Jerry was coached for two years into a higher-level management position. Coaching helped Jerry perform at a higher level; however, the problem was that Jerry simply could not come to terms with the personal conflict he felt at being in the middle. Therefore, he could not consistently perform at a satisfactory level when the situation made him feel caught between staff and management.

Coaching to Confront Poor Performance

No one relishes confronting poor performance. In fact, many supervisors have a tendency to avoid confrontation. Even when the poor performance is seriously affecting customers and coworkers or hurting the effectiveness of the library, supervisors are often slow to deal with it. Why?

For one thing, dealing with poor performance takes time and attention away from other tasks. Just about any work is preferable to documenting, analyzing, and defining the problem performance. Of course, without such data there is no defensible basis for confronting an individual. Confrontation without a well-defined basis for it can be a horrible experience all around and can make things worse. The individual can be angry. He undoubtedly will be if this is the first confrontation in a long history of unchallenged poor performance.

Furthermore, supervisors are often immobilized by what they think will be the consequences of confronting poor performance. What am I causing to happen to this employee? He will resent me. What am I doing to this person's life? What will others think of me? I will feel personally responsible for whatever happens to the individual, and so on. When poor performance has been going on for a long time, how can I make a case if there's no documentation on record? What will it say about me that I don't have a record of the times I've talked with this individual about his performance? The time, the attention, the documentation, and the fear of con-

sequences often influence the supervisor to indefinitely postpone dealing with the poor performance.

Coaching can help a supervisor think through a situation that involves poor performance. The coach helps the supervisor put the situation into perspective. The goal of confronting poor performance is to improve the performance, not to separate someone from his job. The basis for the confrontation need not be onerous; it need only be solid. A coach can help as the supervisor analyzes a performance problem.

Ignoring poor performance won't make it go away. It only makes things worse for the individual, for his self-esteem, for other workers affected by the poor performance, and for organizational morale. To the affected coworkers and subordinates, there are few things more demoralizing than believing that management ignores poor performance. This brings us back to Steve from scenario 9:

> Steve resented having to welcome, orient, and integrate two new staff members; therefore, he withheld information from the newcomers during their initiation. He continued to work independently, essentially ignoring the others. He claimed choice assignments and directed the newcomers to do what was left. He sabotaged the effectiveness of the others by omitting essential information in transmitting assignments. When the program customers began to think that the new staff was unresponsive, Steve did nothing to correct that notion. With coaching from a senior manager, the supervisor eventually confronted Steve's performance.

Anticipating, noticing, and coaching Steve from the outset about his resentment might have averted this problem altogether. However, it is possible that even with coaching, Steve might never have come around to gracefully accepting his new role. The point is that addressing the problem early would have short-circuited the negative effect Steve's resentment had on the new staff and on the services of the unit.

Confronting problem performance early generally averts such unfortunate consequences for the employee, coworkers, and the library. As you saw in the last chapter's application, preparing to confront problem performance is not difficult or excessively time consuming. However, it requires mindfulness and purposefulness on the part of the supervisor.

Coaching into Another Position
or Out of the Organization

At times it makes sense to coach someone into another position or even out of the organization. People change, and their interests and needs change. Organizations change, and the nature of work changes around people. It is not a disgrace or a matter of blame when the person and the job are mismatched. Someone who is perfectly content in a position upon accepting it may want something different five years later. Acknowledging that this change happens and providing coaching for it is a humane response to the normal course of events.

Sometimes, the best thing a coach can do is to help an individual decide on another, more suitable position in the organization or out of it. Take, for example, the situation of Jerry in scenario 4:

> Jerry was stuck in his position and might have stayed, to his and the library's detriment. Jerry's job was literally making him sick, and his performance wasn't working for the library. He spoke of changing careers but could not bring himself to do anything about it. He was immobilized by his fear of leaving the relative security of his position for the unknown. His supervisor understood this and, with an ultimatum, forced Jerry into having to make a choice.

There are times when coaching someone into another position or out of the organization occurs under happier circumstances. Then it is a matter of supporting the decision-making process of someone who wants something different from her current position and is voluntarily pursuing it. Coaches help individuals through the decision-making process, always with the best interests of the individual in mind.

Sometimes, coaching to help someone into another position or out of the organization is also an option for treating a performance problem that coaching cannot correct. The only person who can overcome a performance problem is the individual with the problem. Coaching can help, but the person must cooperate. Look again at the situation presented in scenario 9:

> Steve could not bring himself to work alongside the new staff. Despite his colleagues' repeated attempts to gain his cooperation, Steve simply could not bring himself to accept them as equals. In this case, coaching gave way to a progressive disciplinary process.

Eventually, Steve was offered a choice. He could accept a position in a more traditional work unit or be terminated from employment.

This does not suggest that the indiscriminate or expedient transfer of individuals is a solution to poor performance. Rather, various options must be considered when coaching does not adequately improve poor performance. Coaching is not a solution to every performance problem. The library is not well served by indefinitely coaching a person whose performance remains marginal. The coach must weigh the investment in the person versus the return on the investment for the library.

Poor performance is attributable to many things: poor health, personal stress or crisis, lack of clarity about expectations, the need for training or tutoring, or having to work through a performance barrier such as the resentment that overcame Steve. Poor performance can also signal the individual's disenchantment with the job. This may be something the person cannot change. It may be an indication that the person wants something more or different out of his work.

WHY COACH INDIVIDUALS?

The most important reason to coach individuals is to help them work on the interface of their knowledge, skills, and experience in a changing and somewhat unpredictable environment. Coaching is the organization rolling up its sleeves to help people learn.

Coaching at the individual level makes things better. When you help individuals succeed in their work, they feel better about themselves. They also feel better about working in an organization where individual learning, growing, and improving is encouraged and supported. Ultimately, the overall effectiveness of an organization depends on the performance of each individual in it. There is no getting around this. By coaching individuals, you are helping them and the organization perform at their best.

Individual commitment to the organization is dependent on individuals understanding what is expected and on feedback. Coaching essentially focuses individuals on performance goals. In the process, it clarifies expectations. It provides feedback about performance and helps the individual identify and learn the skills and behaviors that will improve her effectiveness.

Individuals who work in libraries typically want to do a good job. They take pride in their work. They are willing to improve when they understand how their performance falls short of what is needed. To understand means to know in specific, objective terms what is needed and why. When people get this information and feedback as they do in coaching, they feel their supervisor is acting in good faith.

Acting in good faith builds trust, and trust makes workplace relationships durable. Durable working relationships, in turn, enable the organization to hold up under difficult circumstances. Under the best of circumstances—when adequate funding, facilities, equipment, and collections are in place—this durability of working relationships catapults the organization into the realm of the exceptional.

Coaches will need to help people do the things they haven't had to do before. The bar has been raised for library staff at every level. Working collaboratively, managing projects, partnering with the community and industry, and constantly integrating new technology and applications are essential skills of employees at virtually every level of the organization.

In meeting the challenges ahead, library organizations will have a younger and more diversely educated workforce of information professionals and paraprofessionals. Training and coaching paraprofessionals, librarians, and others will be crucial if they are to move into key technical, professional, and managerial positions.

There will be considerable opportunity in libraries for those who want to advance themselves.

Furthermore, there is increasing opportunity for libraries to attract professionals who are not librarians but who are attracted to the library's purpose and mission so they can make a difference in their communities. Those organizations that encourage and support individual growth and development will have an edge over organizations that do not.

HOW TO COACH INDIVIDUALS

Chapter 1, "Coaching Overview," described a framework for the coaching process. In the chapter 2 application, you read the coach's internal dialogue as she prepared to confront Stan's unsatisfactory performance. The following application focuses on the coaching meeting. In it you will see how the coach confronted Stan about his unsatisfactory performance.

No matter how compelling a case the coach makes, coaching cannot be effective without the true cooperation of the player. Coaching cannot be forced. It is the player who actually does the work, makes the improvements, and changes behavior. The coach helps from the sidelines by giving feedback to the player, naming the player's accomplishments, and noting when the player backslides. The coach provides encouragement and an accurate reflection of progress.

This is the type of coaching people ask about most often. The meeting preparation has already taken place. (See the chapter 2 application.) Preparation plus conscious, focused attention to the player and the coach's skillful use of basic coaching will bring Stan and the coach through the meeting in good form.

APPLICATION

COACHING INTERACTION TO CONFRONT POOR PERFORMANCE

Initial Stage

The initial stage of the coaching interaction is when the coach confronts the player with the issue. The player's reaction informs the coach about how to proceed from there. The coach and the player are stating, listening, clarifying, and summarizing. In all stages, the coach attends to the player's emotional well-being.

I greeted Stan, welcomed him into my office, and offered him a chair while I closed the door. We exchanged a few pleasantries as we got settled in our chairs. Stan is generally not one to waste time with small talk, so I began with a little context. I reminded him about what led up to this meeting: the evaluation input process and the strengths and areas for improvement format. He nodded that he understood.

I said, "This meeting is not your performance review meeting. It is an initial meeting to talk with you about what has come up under the 'needs improvement' category. There is a long list of strengths and accolades, and I want you to hear these as well." We agreed to begin with these.

Content Stage

The content stage calls for inquiry, probing, reflecting, and discerning. The coach is actively listening, clarifying, summarizing, and giving feedback while remaining detached, focused, and purposeful. The coach gently but firmly keeps both herself and the player on course. She reasons, analyzes, and resourcefully probes alternatives.

I read the list, intermittently looking at Stan. I wanted to see how Stan was doing. He appeared reserved and poised but formal. As I read the list of strengths and accolades, he wasn't looking directly at me but slightly down and aside. He appeared to be listening thoughtfully to the specific words of appreciation.

When I concluded, Stan said, "It feels good to hear that these people appreciate these things about me. I've never heard these comments before from them. In fact, I haven't received much specific feedback in the time I have been working at the library. Thank you for taking the time to ask for it on my behalf. Now I'm ready to hear the 'needs improvement' part."

I went to my list of behaviors and read them deliberately. Intermittently, I observed Stan's reaction. He listened, appearing thoughtful, and acknowledged that this was familiar territory.

Stan said, "I didn't know all of these people felt this way. I've tried to work things out with those I knew felt this way. I thought things were improving."

I said, "Everyone who responded said they thought you were making an effort to improve. Still, they felt there was room for more improvement." Stan nodded that he had heard me.

I proceeded: "All parties reported being similarly affected by the behaviors. I've made a list of these."

Stan indicated that he was ready to hear the list, so I began to read, pausing between each statement. He showed interest and more facial responsiveness now and appeared intent on listening. He looked dismayed upon hearing some of the effects people reported. I finished the list and paused.

Stan said, "I didn't mean for them to get those messages. For example, I referred Anita to the intranet not because I thought her stupid or incompetent but because I wanted Anita to learn to do her own groundwork. I wanted her to make use of the information that is readily available there."

I acknowledged what Stan said.

Stan continued, "Even so, if this is how people are feeling, it is a problem. I've been working on coming across to people less abruptly, and I'm willing to do more. I've tried to be better at complimenting people about their performance and have taken the time to write e-mails praising them and giving them specific feedback. I guess I don't really know what to do to make this better. Do you have any ideas for what I could do?"

I told him, "I've given this some thought and have some suggestions I'd like to talk with you about. Perhaps we should first clarify the issue—the specific problem—then move into the next steps."

Stan agreed. I began to summarize, checking up on Stan at intervals. I watched to see if he was tracking the gist of what I said.

I summed things up this way: "Stan, you have many qualities that people who work with you uniformly admire. They admire your intelligence, your knowledge, and your ability to produce a great program of service. Your standards are high, you ask a lot of yourself, and you give a lot of yourself to the library. Your staff respects and admires you for this."

Stan acknowledged this.

I went on: "At the same time, your staff is disappointed in their relationships with you. They feel they have been judged by you as inferior and inadequate. You say you do not feel this way about them and that the comments they take as belittling are intended to spur them on to better performance. You believe that the manner in which you communicate your displeasure with others' performances lets them know what you expect. However, the feedback from them indicates that your manner of communicating is received differently than you intend. Stan, the message they take in is that you disapprove of *them*—not of their *behavior*. Your manner of communicating what you want is not working with your staff. What people perceive is your displeasure. You haven't told them what you expect."

I asked Stan if he thought what I said was accurate. He said he was following me and mulling this over. He asked me to keep going.

I continued: "Stan, I believe the problem is this: Your manner of teaching them to do their groundwork is backfiring. They are learning, instead, to be afraid to approach you. They think you disapprove of them. You say you don't intend to convey this."

Stan protested, "I do not disapprove of them. That's not the message I mean to send. What can I do?"

I said, "The method you are using, Stan, is called negative reinforcement. Negative reinforcement punishes undesirable behavior.

Positive reinforcement, on the other hand, rewards desired behavior. If you want them to know that you expect them to do their groundwork, that is what you must tell them. Describe for them what that means to you, and why it is important to you. This is in contrast to being directive. You might do that in your staff meetings and then reinforce this message one-on-one."

Stan said, "I can't imagine how this can reverse how they feel about me."

I could tell that Stan was discouraged. I went on to explain: "Stan, you'll need to reinforce this message from time to time. It takes time for people to relearn. It takes consistent, predictable behavior that they can gradually learn to trust. Yes, it takes time, but that is not in short supply. Your staff think well of you, Stan. We are talking here about working on only one aspect of you, not a major overhaul. Can you see that?"

Stan seemed relieved to be reminded of this. "Yes," he said, "that's right."

Continuing, I said, "I believe it will help remedy the situation if you learn and practice being direct about what you expect in specific terms. This is something to do purposefully in a meeting with those who report to you. Remember that these individuals have learned to be apprehensive about approaching you. Since you have said you don't want this kind of reaction, you will need to be purposeful about reteaching them. You will need to be explicit that you want them to approach you with concerns, ideas, and questions. You will need to reinforce their behavior with corresponding positive feedback.

"There is also the matter of what they have concluded about your opinion of them. This is an issue you might candidly speak with them about. If it isn't what you mean to convey, you could tell them that. You could also tell them what you do think of them, Stan. This must be stated in specific terms. In either case, reflecting on this beforehand will help you have a meaningful interaction with them about this matter."

Stan was intrigued by the concept of positive versus negative reinforcement. He said, "The concept makes sense in theory. Now that I think about it, I believe I actually use positive reinforcement at times. However, what you call negative reinforcement is natural for me. I see

(continued)

that it isn't working, however, and I'm willing to try learning and practicing positive reinforcement."

Wrap-up Stage

What has been resolved, agreements about next steps, and any follow-up that will take place are confirmed at the wrap-up stage. Once the meeting has concluded, the coach makes a brief record of the meeting as a personal reference.

We discussed next steps and concluded that Stan would read up on the topic. He also wants to work with me or another coach in preparation for meeting with his staff. At the meeting he will express his expectations and provide the context for these expectations. Under the tutelage of a coach, he planned to practice positive reinforcement. We agreed upon who this coach will be.

Stan agreed to apply what he was learning in place of using his typical style, and he agreed to begin immediately. We also agreed that it is OK for either of us to check in with the other informally at any time about how this was going. Stan said that he will talk with me if questions or concerns arise for him about positive reinforcement. We scheduled a formal progress check-in in two months.

Stan was able to hear and consider what his coach described: Stan's behaviors, their effect on subordinates, and the conclusion those subordinates had drawn. The coach did not judge or blame; she was the messenger. She used examples of incidents, words, and phrases from the testimony of the subordinates. Stan did not actually concede that his performance was poor. However, he did acknowledge that there was a problem—one that he did not fully understand. He said he was willing to work on it. Although he had not meant to be demeaning or dismissive, he was concerned about the effect. He was also open to the possibility that there was a better way to communicate and was willing to be tutored and further coached.

This chapter and its application have shown the various ways coaching can help individual performance and ultimately organizational effectiveness. There are many opportunities to reintroduce meaningful interaction about the work of the library. This meaningful interaction at the level of supervisor-to-employee engages individuals as nothing else can.

This chapter has presented many reasons for coaching individuals. With so many opportunities to coach, basic coaching skills obviously belong in the tool kit of every supervisor. These skills include effective listening, skillful feedback, and understanding and applying the process stages of coaching. Even the dreaded act of confronting poor or lagging performance can be effectively addressed with a modest amount of focused attention, planning, and the effective application of basic coaching skills.

4 coaching teams

COACHING individuals is one thing, but coaching teams is another. Teams of individuals are doing more and more work in libraries. How does coaching come into play when performance depends on not one but several individuals? In this chapter, we shall discover the essential differences in coaching teams and how individual coaching relates to team effectiveness.

PRELUDE

As I observe the meeting, I ponder the difference in this library's management team since several weeks ago. Until now these talented individuals seemed to have been going it alone, even though they are ostensibly part of a team. Their meetings had a competitive edge. Individuals were typically quiet or critical or boastful. If anything was troubling any of these managers, they did not say. No one expressed a need for help.

Now the difference is notable. The meeting is upbeat and purposeful. The team seems confident, and the meeting agenda is relevant. Everyone seems to know what to do today in the meeting. They are engaged; that is, they are prepared, listening, and contributing. They discipline themselves to the agenda, but there is ease, laughter, and accommodation. Interaction is respectful and good-natured. It is clear that work has been done ahead of the meeting to enable decisions to be made here. The meeting ends with an air of accomplishment and on time! This team has changed. Individuals are not coming to a meeting out of obligation—they are moving as one with a purpose.

A group of people does not make a team. Experience at work and elsewhere in life has taught us this. We see this in our library work units at every level of the organization. Naming a group a team does not make it one. A group saying that it is a team does not make it one, either. For instance, a group of managers is not a team just because they call themselves a management team and meet together regularly. A work unit may call itself a team when it is actually more like an armed camp. Effective, high-performance teams have structure and operate under conditions that enable the team to perform effectively.

A team can gain no collective forward momentum without a shared, conscious purpose. Their meetings may provide a venue for seeing one another, reestablishing contact, exchanging information, and occasionally making a collective decision. However, without a purposeful, expressed reason to be, they are not a team.

A team
- has and is committed to a common purpose
- has leadership
- uses the talents of all of its members to accomplish its purpose
- knows to attend to the well-being of all members of the team
- finishes the game together

A team is able to accomplish what groups of people cannot because team members have a purposeful commitment to something they have put ahead of self-interest. Teamwork is purposeful interdependency, which has the synergistic effect of accomplishing more than the sum of the parts.

WHAT IT MEANS TO COACH TEAMS

Achieving a common purpose through collaboration with others is a unique work experience. Individuals working effectively together for a common purpose create a force: a *power to perform*. The team power to perform makes the effort compelling, engrossing, and fun. Team members are in this together. Each member is known and appreciated for what that individual can do. There is tolerance for the inevitable mistakes team members are bound to make. Individuals have room to move around and be who they are because teammates know what each brings to the team. Each develops a belief in himself or herself and the team. Individuals know they can deal with whatever comes along because the team will find a way. In fact, there is unbounded potential in the team to make something amazing happen.

The measure of a team's effectiveness is whether it can efficiently accomplish its purpose with the team's and each individual's self-esteem intact. Team coaching often focuses on process because

it is in process that teamwork often gets bogged down. The role of the coach is to help create and sustain the conditions under which teams are generally effective.

As with coaching individuals, a team may take a little or a lot of coaching, depending on the circumstances. Coaching may be short term or long term. The level and extent of coaching depends upon the number and complexity of the coaching goals.

In one situation, coaching may be only a matter of helping the team clarify why it is floundering. The objective observation and inquiry of the coach helps the team clear a hurdle, maybe in just one meeting. For example, individual team members can easily get caught up in their own agendas and lose sight of the team goal. The coach, observing from the sidelines, recognizes that this has happened and sees what is needed to get the team back on track by asking the right questions.

Another situation may call for having the coach in the wings through most or all of an entire team process. For example, this approach may be needed when some of the team's work is very hard. Libraries that are venturing into cross-functional teamwork and self-managing teams, for instance, are finding that the learning curve is steep and fraught with difficulty and frustration. Assigning, hiring, or borrowing a coach to help in this situation will save time and reduce frustration and disillusionment all around.

The Substance of Team Coaching

Coaches help individuals build their skills for teamwork. They help teams who are derailed get back on track. They help those who commission teams and those who serve on them improve team effectiveness and efficiency.

Building Skills
For the good of the library, staff members need to be able to work together effectively. Individuals from across several work units are frequently drawn together to plan a service or resolve a service problem. For instance, when it is time for a library to replace its integrated library system (ILS), stakeholders from information technology, reference, collections, and circulation services must all be at the table together. Leaders and managers expect others to work effectively as part of teams, committees, task forces, and work units.

While library personnel are becoming more practiced at working together, this is not essentially how people in libraries are accustomed to working or what they are accustomed to seeing among leaders and managers. Coaching helps individuals, teams, leaders, and managers work together efficiently and productively and to become more discerning about when to form teams.

Coaches help individuals build interpersonal skills and teams build process skills. After all, being part of a team makes additional demands on the individual and requires collaborative skills. Asking someone who has worked solo to work in a team is like asking a solo violinist to play in an orchestra when she has only played solo. Coaches often help individuals who are unaccustomed to working in teams understand what it means and what it will take from them to have a successful experience and to contribute to a successful outcome. Coaches help individuals and teams, leaders and managers develop their interpersonal, collaborative, and process skills.

Back on Track

Sometimes coaches discover that a team is struggling. This happens for a variety of reasons. Often, it is because the team's assignment is ill defined or really doesn't call for a team. Managers typically feel they already have too much to do themselves, and, other than using a team, there may be no one to whom they can delegate a particular issue. Sometimes there are more of these particular issues than managers can handle, but there is pressure from above and below to do something about them. Passing issues on to a team can be a temporary relief for a burdened manager because it feels like work is getting done just to dispatch the assignment! Of course, it is a start, but it can also be premature and a setup for team failure.

Whatever the reasons, the result often is that the team struggles with an assignment it is ill equipped to complete successfully. Time is wasted, and people become soured on teamwork and resentful of the people who put them there. Coaching can help identify when this is happening or, better yet, avert the situation altogether. Coaching helps those who commission teams become more discerning about when to team up.

Coaches find that it is the thorny issues that often get handed off to a team. Thorny issues tend to fall into one of three categories: technology, niggling policy, or broken processes. Such issues get assigned to an existing committee or to a special task force or team because "several heads are better than one." Sometimes dispatching the work to a team, however, is a knee-jerk reaction to a confounding problem.

Resource Allocation Issues and Teams

Sometimes the issue needs to be managed not by a team but by a manager. For instance, rather than appoint a team in scenario 10 of chapter 1, a different manager's approach to the headset dilemma might have been to make a decision based on the input of a few key informants on both sides of the issue. On the other hand, this particular manager wanted the staff involved to experience working through a stalemate because similar issues had come up before and would again. This manager believed it was in her best interest if the staff learned how to resolve such issues. She was willing to put time in, up front, to coach the team through a team learning process.

Teams are not equipped to handle some of the things they are asked to do. Perhaps it is that the assignment is just very hard for this team or for any team. It may be that the task requires too much effort from people who are already doing too many other things. Coaches help managers learn to objectively weigh an assignment that is under consideration. How much will this teamwork cost? How will taking on this assignment affect the productivity of the team members? What will be delayed or not accomplished by making this assignment? Who will be affected by the delays, and how much will they be affected?

Coaches help libraries get the most from teams. Many libraries use teams a great deal. Libraries are learning how to do this, and people are learning from participating in teamwork. Teaming people up to grapple with challenging service issues, even if the process is inefficient by some standards, gives many people a place at the learning table. Clerks, pages, other support staff, and the non-MLS professionals are increasingly sitting at the table of library-purpose-and-planning discussions. This is beneficial for them and for the organization.

Is using teams in this way a good stewardship of resources? For some organizations, the inclusion and learning are worth the cost. Others feel they cannot afford it or are beyond it. That is, they feel they have learned their lessons, that individuals and the library have benefited, and they are fine-tuning processes for greater efficiency. The answer is different for each library, and the answer changes as the organization evolves. Essentially, libraries benefit when individuals who work in them know how to work easily and effectively together. Strengthening this ability enables the organization to respond more effectively, but this is achieved at the cost of time, and time is money.

The choice about where to place responsibility for the work must be a thoughtful one. When individuals commission teams, they are committing valuable resources. If they do this well, they avoid souring people on teamwork. We are always teaching, whether we mean to or not. If we are purposeful about teams, team members learn that teamwork can be enriching and productive. If we are careless about teams, we are teaching people that teamwork hurts.

Who Coaches Teams?

Supervisors and managers, in particular, must be able to coach teams. Other resources for team coaching include external consultants who specialize in coaching. Libraries may turn to the outside for coaching when the internal coaching resources are stretched thin or when the situation calls for a level of expertise that is not available within the library. The library's parent organization, for example, may supply this expertise. Libraries can build the expertise internally, too. Some organizations or their parent institutions provide training for coaching. Any individual who wants to can coach teams if he or she is willing to develop the basic skills and characteristics of an effective coach and understands what makes teams work.

Conditions Influencing Team Performance

Five interdependent conditions influence team performance:

1. The assignment is well defined, and the team must understand the assignment.
2. The team has the talent and team skills to accomplish the assignment.
3. The team has effective leadership for accomplishing the assignment.
4. The team has the resources it needs to accomplish the assignment.

5. The team members collaboratively, skillfully, and persistently apply their talents to achieve the team's goals.

Ideally, these five conditions are mindfully set in place when the team first forms and meets. More often, the coach is called in to help an existing team that is floundering. When teams flounder, it is often because one or more of the five conditions does not exist. Coaching can help the team create and sustain these conditions over the course of the assignment. The following sections take a closer look at each of these conditions.

Condition 1

The assignment is well defined, and the team must understand the assignment. Without a common purpose, there is no team. The common purpose should be set forth in a written statement. It may be written for an existing group or be developed as an assignment for a newly formed team. This chapter's application shows how a management team creates a common agenda, organizes around it, and thereby refocuses on its purpose.

Ideally, the team's assignment is developed before the team begins to work. In real life, this does not usually happen. Typically, the team develops a statement or understanding of its purpose later, after they have floundered a while. This can happen if the team was formed before its assignment was clearly developed. In reality, a team often begins without a clear idea of what it is supposed to accomplish. The sooner the team can define its purpose, desired outcomes, and parameters, the better—because valuable time, energy, and goodwill of the team can otherwise be eroded. This is where the coach can help.

The coach guides this process of developing the team's statement of purpose or coaches a team leader to do so. The coach also helps the person who assigns the team to clarify the objective. This is generally someone who has a primary stake in the matter: the director, a manager, a subset of a larger team, or a small team of two or three interested individuals.

The coach elicits the objective by asking clarifying questions. The result is a concise statement of the issue, including the desired outcome of the work to be undertaken. The statement includes any parameters, givens, or limitations that must be taken into account and an approximation of the level of effort to be allotted and the expected completion date.

Overall, the assignment should be challenging but realistic. Its difficulty or complexity must not outstrip the talent or time of the individuals who might constitute the team. Furthermore, the work must warrant forming a team.

The coach asks about the interests of key stakeholders and informants. It is generally useful for the assignment to be developed with their input. Stakeholders are those or representatives of those who will be affected by the outcome of the work; for instance, the customers, staff, and policy makers. Stakeholders have crucial information to help define the issue and the desired results. Key informants are those who have technical expertise to help scope out the assignment, its parameters, assumptions, and limitations. As the following example shows, the stakeholders and informants are drawn from many diverse groups.

> The assignment is to evaluate and recommend an open source (OS) integrated online system that outperforms the library's commercial ILS. An OS team will be created. There are several stakeholder groups: the public users, the public services staff, the technical services staff, and the information technology staff. They have a stake in the outcome of the project. They are also resources for the team, providing their various perspectives as well as technical expertise.

Hearing or reading the written assignment is just the beginning of understanding it. It is important to bring the team together initially and inform members about the work ahead. This grounds the team. For instance, a team orientation meeting focuses the team on the reason they are together. They learn why they have been chosen and what they are expected to accomplish. They have an opportunity to listen and ask questions. They hear the context for the assignment. Through dialogue comes a shared understanding of the assignment, parameters, givens, and limitations. The context and the reasoning behind the assignment are clarified. Hearing why individuals have been chosen for an assignment personalizes it and helps the team buy into the project. When a team has floundered, it is frequently because the team members have lost focus. The leader refocuses the team on its purpose throughout the process.

Condition 2

The team has the talent and team skills to accomplish the assignment. What knowledge, skills, and abilities are needed to accomplish the assignment? The answers guide the selection of the team members. Leadership is at the top of any team list. Who will be able to understand the assignment, develop a process strategy, and facilitate the team process? Who will be able to keep the team focused as well as energized and engaged? Who will be able to ensure that an atmosphere of mutual respect and individual self-esteem is maintained?

The team members must be able to put purpose and team well-being ahead of self-interest. Interpersonal maturity is a major factor in team performance. Strong team players are people who can listen. They understand that other people can offer something worth hearing. Those with interpersonal maturity can put themselves in another's shoes, follow through on what they agree to do, and attend to the other team members.

Special skills and abilities will be needed in the project, so those skills are considerations in selecting the team.

> For efficiency, the team will be as small as possible. It must have the right stakeholders as well as those with practical and technical expertise. Therefore, choosing those who have team skills as well as the ability to appreciate others' perspectives will narrow the field of choices.

The need for technical expertise, practical experience, certain personal attributes, and team skills influences the team selection. Some of the stakeholders and resource people may be right for the team. Team composition has a political as well as a practical dimension: getting buy-in from certain sectors of the organization is often a political objective that influences team appointments. Individuals often come to the team with their own agendas. This is all the more reason to be clear about the assignment and the expectations of team members.

Condition 3

The team has effective leadership for accomplishing the assignment. Effective leadership is indispensable to team success. It is the team leader/facilitator who minds the overall project purpose and parameters. The leader brings the team back to its purpose, clarifies the project, and regroups and refocuses the members as needed. She minds process and helps design an effective approach to accomplishing the assignment. She attends to the overall well-being of the team.

A lot can happen in a team to hinder its performance. For example, factions can develop within the team because members are at odds on a key point and are unable to get past the stalemate. It might be the team leader herself who is dominating the process and stifling the team's productivity. Therefore, the coach might coach the team leader or perhaps one or more members of the team.

It is essential to have a team leader or facilitator who has the ability to help the team organize itself for the work to be accomplished. Efficiency is one of the measures of an effective team. The leader must be able to focus the team and move the process along without quashing the team's spirit and creativity.

Even a competent team leader or facilitator can be stymied at times in the process. The performance barriers presented in figure 1.1 come into play in teams. For example, one of the team members may have an overactive ego. He may frequently interrupt meetings with stories of his accomplishments, ostensibly to emphasize a point someone has made. This uses the team's time in the meeting and interferes with the momentum of the team.

Ideally, someone on the team will know how to handle such a barrier effectively. However, teams often don't know what to do about this barrier. People often get angry or nervously skirt the behavior. The behavior, however, is drawing their attention away from the work at hand. A clumsy attempt to correct the situation might sound like this:

> "If Leon would stop grandstanding, we could make some progress here."

A coach can help the team facilitator see Leon's behavior as only human. The coach knows the leader must bring this person's skills to the work at hand. Just saying what is needed from Leon is usually enough to refocus him:

> "Leon, you have some wonderful stories. However, the team really needs your listening and focused contributions. It will help if you hold the stories for another time."

Condition 4
The team has the resources it needs to accomplish the assignment. The team members themselves—their time and talent—are the major resources for accomplishing the assignment. Time is money, as the saying goes. The time spent in and out of meetings on the assignment adds up fast.

Teams usually need more resources than just the abilities and interests of the team members. For example, the team needs a clear assignment and the authority to carry it out. The team's purpose and authority may be announced within the organization in a formal notice, which helps the team get the attention and cooperation of others in the organization. Another important resource is that of a sponsor—a powerful person in the organization who can help the team break through the bureaucracy. This might be a manager, a senior manager, the director, or some other highly placed person. The sponsor may also be a resource to help the team reclarify its purpose. The sponsor may be active or may wait in the wings until the team asks for his help.

Teams may need financial resources or the authority to make commitments for the library. If so, the team needs to know the extent of that authority. The team may need to call in experts to help with aspects of the assignment, for example. What are the conditions under which the team may do this? Who must authorize this?

A coach is another resource. Teams may need a coach to help them in the beginning or at intervals in the process. The coach helps bring about the conditions that enable team effectiveness.

Condition 5
The team members collaboratively, skillfully, and persistently apply their talents to achieve the team's goals. Like all work, teamwork thrives in an atmosphere of generosity, reliability, compassion, and courage. This atmosphere engenders trust among team members. Trust enables the team to make progress. It releases people from self-consciousness, permitting more creativity and risk-taking.

All of the performance barriers (see figure 1.1) that can be at play in individual coaching can also be present in a team, and in infinite combination. This can make it difficult to figure out what is going wrong, because lots of things can be wrong simultaneously. For instance, someone may continually fail to meet agreements the team members have made about the work schedule. Another individual's ego may be overinvolved in one of the team tasks. One team member who waits her turn may resent the team member who rarely does. Another may insist on withholding her work until her teammate produces his. Weak accountability, weak egos, interpersonal immaturity, either/or thinking—all of these individual performance barriers can make a team leader want to run away. Individual coaching comes into play when the team is floundering due to one or more individuals' performance.

WHY COACH TEAMS?

Coaching helps individuals and groups learn how to function effectively and successfully in teams. Many people are not accustomed to working collaboratively. Even the willing person becomes frustrated with teamwork, for teamwork invariably bogs down at times. Coaching helps the team quickly isolate a team problem and get back on track.

Coaching helps teams resolve problems and challenges better and more efficiently in the workplace. It also helps individuals on teams learn to handle normal workplace interpersonal conflict. Individuals and teams can relearn in the workplace that there is life after conflict.

Coaching helps the organization gradually become better at triaging new, difficult, and complex work. It helps leaders become better at deploying these assignments in the organization and to identify the most useful and efficient models for accomplishing work in teams. Finally, coaching helps everyone in the organization become skilled at determining when a team is needed for the work.

HOW TO COACH TEAMS

Coaching is not only a tool for troubleshooting team problems, but is also a tool for team development. The coach uses various tools and techniques for assessing team effectiveness, for diagnosing team turbulence, and for developing teams.

Coaching Assessment Tools

The coach can use the five conditions influencing team performances and the ten performance factors listed in figure 1.1 as assessment tools. Remember that a team problem may be structural. That is, it may be related to the five conditions influencing team performance. It may also stem from the performance of one or more players. One or more

performance barriers can be affecting an individual or the team as a whole. The problem may present itself as either a performance issue or as a structural issue, but it may actually be stemming from the other. The coach, of course, is looking for the root cause.

Starting a team well means that the five conditions influencing team performance are in place. Coaching managers can influence this throughout the organization because they often appoint or authorize a team assignment. They can ponder the appropriateness of having a team versus a manager, individual, or work unit do the assignment. Without the five conditions in place, teams will struggle unnecessarily or fail altogether.

When diagnosing team turbulence, the coach mentally visits the five conditions influencing team performance and asks questions like these:

1. *Is the assignment well defined? Does the team understand the assignment?*
   Is the team's purpose spelled out?
   Does it make sense?
   Is it realistic, even if it is challenging?
   Is the team clear about its purpose?

2. *Does the team have effective leadership for accomplishing the assignment?*
   Is the team's approach to the assignment reasonable and realistic?
   Is the team's process logical? Is it efficient?
   Is there something in the team's approach to this work that is thwarting its progress? If so, what is it?
   What is behind the team's decision to take its particular approach to the work?
   Are the team's assumptions leading the team offtrack?
   Has the team checked out these assumptions with the person who can verify them?
   Is the team focused on its purpose?

3. *Does the team have the talent and team skills to accomplish the assignment?*
   Does the team have the experience and talent to do this?
   Is somebody missing who could fill a gap if he or she could join the team or be a team resource?
   Are the team players skilled in teamwork?

4. *Does the team have the resources it needs to accomplish the assignment?*

   Is the team making steady progress?

   Does it seem to be blocked from making progress? If so, what is the nature of the barrier? Is it something in the team's control and if not, who does control it?

   Does the team need to be encouraged to seek clarification?

   Has something changed since the work began that should influence an alteration in the assignment or some crucial precept of the assignment?

5. *Do the team members collaboratively, skillfully, and persistently apply their talents to achieve the team's goals?*

   Is everyone contributing?

   Is something going on interpersonally with the group?

   Is the group in conflict? If so, what is the nature of it?

   Is the team goal still at center stage or are individual agendas distracting the team from its purpose?

   Did the assignment developer misjudge the talent? If so, how? What can be done about it?

   Is the team discouraged? If so, why?

Inevitably teams will have some difficulty. When a team is having difficulty, members won't necessarily know why or what to do. Checking back in with the team, especially as the team is launched and at key checkpoints along the way, is time well invested in the team's success. The coach follows up on signs of team turbulence. Indications of problems may be an offhand comment, a missed deadline, or a product delay, for example. The coach is mindful of the team and its progress. He has an agreement with the team about how and under what circumstances he should be summoned; then he is responsive to the call.

In this chapter's prelude, you were with the coach as she observed the management team meeting. She was struck by the change in the team from the way they had worked together several weeks before. What happened that brought about such a difference in this team? The following application is the coach's analysis of the team turbulence she observed several weeks before. The treatment plan for the team obviously worked. In this application you will discover what essentially was not working and what changed the scenario. As you will see in this chapter's application, a little coaching goes a long way. It often takes little time to listen and provide feedback to help the team get back on course.

APPLICATION

THE MANAGEMENT TEAM DEFINES ITS PURPOSE AND ORGANIZES AROUND IT

The management team, made up of the senior managers of the library's major divisions and the library director, had been meeting every week. The team became unhappy with its meetings. Again and again, the team revisited why it meets and whether the meetings are worth the time they take. The team experimented with meeting less frequently, more frequently, and not at all.

The team could not seem to come to terms about what it should do at the meetings. It experimented with a variety of formats. It grappled with its purpose: should the meetings be decision-making or informational? Was the team the decision-making body, or was it advisory to the director? If the director did not run the meetings, who should? Who should attend, what should be done, how frequently should they meet? Must the director be present? These questions resurfaced again and again from the team members.

Observation

The coach observed several team meetings. She also interviewed the members of the team. These were the coach's observations:

Meeting Observations

Individuals came into the meeting room, set down their belongings, then left again to do one more thing while others arrived. Some wrote agenda items on the flip chart grouped under priority 1, priority 2, and priority 3. With the coming and going of team members, the meetings did not begin on time. The "priority level" of agenda items on the flip chart established the agenda sequence. The high-priority items included those that needed immediate action. Priorities 2 and 3 were less pressing.

The facilitator, seated at one end of a long, rectangular table, always began the meetings by referring to the agenda and asking if there were additional items. Some usually were added. He always began with the priority 1 items—informational items and instructions about things that must be done right away. The facilitator worked his way through the items, calling on those who put them on the list. Team members asked questions and made remarks about what was said. The facilitator moved the group on to the next item and then to the next category. He checked off the items as they were dispatched. Intermittently, he observed the time and moved the group along when they were lingering too long over a topic. Usually about halfway through the allotted meeting time, he would announce a ten-minute break and ask everyone to return on time.

During the break, some people would leave while others talked in twosomes, intent over calendars or quickly catching up with each other. At the appointed time, some people returned; others returned and left again to check their e-mail.

The facilitator called the meeting to order, absent some members. He picked up where he had left off with the agenda.

At the last meeting one of the members who returned late appeared agitated and took her seat. The facilitator continued without pause. After a few minutes, another member apologized for interrupting the agenda and drew attention to the still-agitated individual. She asked, "Is something going on? If there is, is it something the group can help you with?"

The agitated person explained, "I got bad news during the break—there's been a key resignation. The person left for a more lucrative job."

Some individuals around the table expressed sympathy while others asked about details of the departing person's new job. Then the group began lamenting the sorry compensation package at the library. They felt that this resignation would surely result in more resignations and difficulty in hiring as well. This led to remarks and protestations relating to the hiring process,

(continued)

the competitiveness of jobs at the library, and what the library should do in the future to avoid a repetition of this unfortunate situation. Side conversations took place, and many minutes elapsed.

The facilitator drew attention to the time and how much of the agenda remained. The group quieted and was led by the facilitator through the remainder of the priority 2 items. The facilitator said there was only time enough left to build the agenda for the next meeting. The priority 3 items, he noted, would be carried over until the next meeting. The meeting adjourned. Some people gathered around the agitated member to talk further. Others left the meeting room.

Interviews

In individual interviews of the team members, the coach asked the following questions:

- How satisfied are you with the management team meetings, on a five-point scale?
- What do you think is and is not working with the team?
- What works for you, and what does not work for you?
- Do you think this team needs to meet, and if so, why?
- What do you want out of the meeting?
- What do you think the organization needs from these meetings?

The interviews revealed that satisfaction with the meetings rated below three on a five-point scale for everyone.

The list of what worked was brief. For example, "It works to have a facilitator and a recorder and to meet weekly."

The list of what did not work was much longer. The items on this list had to do with behaviors of various team members during the meeting. For example, "It does not work when (so-and-so) dominates the discussion." "It does not work that the meeting becomes competitive." "It does not work to bring something to the team, because asking for comment triggers a critical feeding frenzy."

Most team members thought the team needed to meet. However, some were doubtful that it should meet, because the meetings were unproductive. In answer to why the team should meet, most agreed that sharing information, seeing one another regularly, and occasionally making policy decisions were reasons the team should meet.

What people said they wanted personally from the meeting varied. However, there were some common themes: hearing important information from one another about what was going on in the organization was important. Regularly seeing other managers, hearing about priorities, and getting directions from the director were also important.

The last question stumped most of the team. Some said that what the organization needed out of the management team meetings was leadership. When asked how the meetings would provide this, no one knew.

Diagnosis

After looking at the information gathered through observations and interviews, the coach made the following diagnosis:

The interviews and meeting visits revealed a great deal about the team's condition. The team's troubles were largely attributable to the first of the five conditions influencing team performance: the team did not have a common purpose that had either been defined for the team or that the team had defined for itself. Thus, the team had nothing to focus it; it did not have an expressed reason to exist that all team members agreed upon. A secondary issue for this team was that the designated leader had no vision for the team and, therefore, was not equipped to lead the team in formulating its purpose. Another member of the team with a vision for the team might be able to engage the others around that vision, develop a game plan, and with a common agenda, enable meaningful interaction. The lack of purpose and the independent views of what the meetings should accomplish left the team members disengaged.

The management team had not settled on a collective purpose. Of course, these individuals had management responsibilities within the same library. However, when they met, they did so as individual managers, not as a team with a common purpose. In the abstract, they were the management team for the library, but what was it they intended to accomplish in the next year or so? What were they uniquely authorized and singularly responsible to do for this organization in that time frame? What in the organization needed their collective attention and effort in the immediate future? As the management team, what must they accomplish on behalf of the organization?

Not only had the team not agreed on its purpose, it lacked a leadership vision. There was leadership potential in the group, but no one had stepped forward to focus the group on its purpose. Therefore, the team was unsure about what to do at its meetings, and the meetings were predominantly informational. The substantive issues were usually carried over into subsequent meetings repeatedly, never getting the attention of the team.

Performance barriers for the team included lack of boundaries, doing the wrong work, and weak accountability. The coach recorded the following symptoms of these barriers:

There was little evidence of advanced meeting planning or preparation by the team members outside the meeting. The team members consistently did not follow through on agreements at one meeting to come prepared to the next. This weak accountability has become accepted practice in the team.

The facilitator and not the group took responsibility for the meeting and for the effective use of time in the meeting. Individuals were late for meetings and returned late from breaks. The group had no agreements about how they would work together in the meeting. Some individuals made remarks that seemed intended to amuse or impress but were not useful in processing an agenda item.

Ending on time was a high priority among the team members. Little work was done outside the meetings by either the facilitator or the team members to prepare for the meeting. With so much to do, most seemed very wary of time in meetings. There was frustration with the group process, even irritation and distaste for having to be at the meetings with the team. If the team could not be productive, then individuals felt they could at least get back to their work.

Prognosis

Although the team was "out of condition," the data from the coach's observations suggested that the prognosis for this team was good to excellent. The following are her thoughts on the matter:

These individuals want to work together. They have easily identified substantive issues that need their attention. There is strong leadership ability on the team. There is a diversity of talent and styles among the members. They appear to like being with each other. The team has many resources at its disposal.

At this point, the coach effectively used the coaching level two-by-two to think through the level of coaching that would help put this team back on track. The coach thought:

The team puts a high value on its time, and the amount of time spent in meetings has been a concern to everyone. At the same time, it is important for the team to get on course—and the sooner the better. Team members are willing to put time in up front to get organized for the sake of gaining efficiencies later. The team also feels that some of its work is more important than other work. Therefore, I'll make the two-by-two axes variables "now/later" and "more important/less important."

With some coaching, the team should be able to develop a statement of purpose and common agenda for the next twelve to eighteen months. They will also need to devise a structure for their work together. The substantive issues they have identified will take work outside the allotted meeting time. However, the meetings will be the right venue for briefings and decisions, with work outside leading up to these. The members of the team respect one another. The stylistic differences in the group can be managed with ground rules the team decides upon.

(continued)

Some brush-up on communication skills and on disciplined practice will strengthen the team relationships.

In the short term, a common agenda, a structure for accomplishing that agenda, ground rules, and skills brushup will put this team on course. Longer term, the group needs a committed team leader to keep the team focused on purpose, goals, and continuing development of the team. The team will need to experience consistency and success under this new model. Each member will need to give more focused time and attention to the work of the team. Individual commitment to developing the interpersonal skills within the team will strengthen the resiliency of the team.

Treatment

Reflecting on the strategies that could help this team, the coach saw how to immediately help it. She paid particular attention to her two-by-two notes, especially on the short-term quadrants. The coach planned the following treatment:

The group will have two to three focused work sessions within a thirty-day period. The purpose of the work sessions will be to develop a statement of purpose, a common agenda, and a structure for the team. The team will designate a leader for a fixed period of time. The group will designate a team member to organize these work sessions with the aid of a coach.

Answering the following questions will help the team in this process.

- Apart from your individual managerial responsibilities, what items in the organization need this particular team's attention?
- What priority do these items have?
- What do you, as individuals, want from this team?
- What do you need to have happen at the team's meetings to make it worthwhile for you as a manager?

Results

The team had the focused work sessions. The members successfully identified a statement of purpose, a common agenda, and priorities. They designated a team leader for a six-month period. Outside the meeting, a subteam developed a proposed team structure for accomplishing the work. This structure included establishing meeting frequency, duration, and locations; establishing protocols for team communication; and designating a team leader.

Mindful that their time spent in meetings is an expensive proposition, the team organized themselves for efficiently expediting the work. Four subteams would tackle the most complex four issues over the course of twelve to eighteen months. This work would be accomplished outside the regular monthly meetings of the whole team. They would come back to the whole team at key decision points. To ensure a shared understanding of that work, each subteam prepared a brief summary of its work plan. This included a statement of the work, the approach or methodology, the expected outcome, and the timeline. The whole team thoughtfully examined and adopted these brief work plans at a management team meeting. The team authorized the subteams to proceed. The management team's calendar of meetings docketed the subteams for updates, coincident to key decision points.

The team began to coalesce. Now they were asking themselves what else they wanted from their meetings and from the team. They adopted some team ground rules—agreements for conducting themselves in meetings so the meetings would work for the team. They also decided to refresh their communication skills together. They set aside three of their meetings over a quarter year for this purpose and hired a coach to conduct the training. The coach worked with them individually and together as they practiced their communication skills with one another. They agreed to evaluate the team's effectiveness at six-month intervals.

5 coaching leaders

THE LIBRARY organization is also a team—a very large team—and, as the preceding application demonstrated, leadership is a powerful team influence. In this chapter, we will look at what it means to coach leaders, why leaders need coaching, and how to coach leaders.

PRELUDE

Imagine yourself in the press box overlooking a football game in progress. Down on the field you see the library director with a few library players in a huddle. Everyone else from the library is standing on the sidelines. A few people are in the stands.

There are only minutes left to play, and the stakes are high. The library players are struggling; they are behind in the game. They are up against some really tough competition. They need more library players on the field. They gesture frantically for players from the sidelines, but the people on the sidelines are afraid to get into the game. They haven't played much, and they're not in shape. They don't know the game plan or the plays. Some of them really want to play, but they are intimidated and afraid.

The fans are shouting, "Defense, defense!" The few other players are defending the director, but the competition is pressing to sack him. The bench is hollering, "Pass! Pass!" But there is no one down the field to receive the ball. The director heaves a "Hail Mary" toward the end zone. Those on the sidelines gape in worried expectation.

This allegory symbolizes what library leaders experience amidst the changes that engulf the institutions they lead. They are in a high-stakes game. The goal is to ensure library institutional viability in a burgeoning, competitive information marketplace. In this marketplace, consumers will eventually have many other options for services that were traditionally the province of the library. To be viable in that developing marketplace, library organizations must be highly effective.

The ultimate proof of leadership effectiveness is a community of stakeholders that are committed to an excellent library. Whether yours is an academic, public, school, or special library, the bottom-line performance indicators are the same: the community uses, prizes, and financially supports the really effective library.

WHAT IT MEANS TO COACH LEADERS

The most essential shaper of library success is the library director. It is the library director, after all, who is constantly marshaling the resources to build and sustain a viable library for the community. The director is ultimately responsible for the myriad of relationships that inspire and sustain an internal and external commitment to library excellence. It is the library director to whom everyone looks for the library vision.

However, the leadership of the organization consists of and takes more than a library director. Good leadership must constantly percolate throughout the organization to achieve a high-performance library.

There is a hierarchy of leadership, of course, with a director at the top of the hierarchy in most libraries. Likewise, the library director is part of the leadership system of the parent organization. That is, the director represents the university, school district, city, or state by virtue of his or her position as a leader in that system.

The collective leadership of designated and undesignated leaders throughout an organization makes up the leadership system. Even as leaders function seemingly independently, their messages and actions convey what leaders stand for. Leaders may think of themselves as acting independently, but in fact what they do and say contributes to an overall leadership posture that can make the institution better or worse. There is no neutral ground, especially for leaders. The leaders of an organization, together, determine what the organization stands for. The library leadership is responsible for seeing to the overall health of the leadership system. They have to be willing to work on this.

For leadership to work powerfully, it needs to be present throughout the organization. This leadership presence happens through others who, for better or worse, convey what the leadership expects, what the leadership cares about, and where the leadership is headed.

Who Are Library Leaders?

Organizations have both designated and natural leaders. The designated leaders are the library director, managers, and other individuals who are explicitly assigned leadership roles. Natural leaders are those who, regardless of position or title, have the ability to influence others (for better or worse). This chapter is about coaching both designated and natural leaders.

Today library leaders are concerned about successors. They talk about "growing" future leaders and about "leading from any position." They ask individuals at every level of the organization to serve in leadership roles as team leaders, project leaders, process leaders, and community leaders.

They understand that they need to fan out leadership in their organizations and communities and that the leadership in an organization cannot be the singular responsibility of the library director or even of a senior management team. Too much is changing and too much needs to be done to leave it to one person. To coach leaders means to help develop the leadership that is needed throughout the organization.

The character of leadership is understood by what the leadership system has running through its veins. If senior leaders are unclear about the library's vision, the rest of the organization will also be unclear about the vision. If the leadership is overly focused on short-term gain, then so goes the rest of the organization. If the leadership is insensitive to the development of individuals in the workplace, the rest of the organization will be. Likewise, if the leadership is imbued with the library's vision, balances short-term and long-term gain, and is committed to the development of others, these values will be apparent throughout the ranks of the organization.

The Challenge of Identifying Natural Leaders

One of the challenges of coaching leaders is identifying who are natural leaders in the library. Natural leaders, some of whom are also designated leaders, are people that other people listen to. They are the people whom others ask, "What do you think we should do about this?" The natural leader's answer is one that others pay attention to.

Leadership is a group issue. Natural leaders are defined by the way people treat them. They are the ones that others go to for advice and who always seem to have things figured out. They are inquisitive and interested in what is going on around them. Generally, they have a compelling personality, which is not to say that this is always positive.

However, there is something magnetic about natural leaders. They are generally observant and interested; therefore, people tend to seek them out.

Natural leaders think of and say things that other people haven't thought of or said. This is compelling and inspires confidence in the leader. Natural leaders generally want to be involved, and they find ways to become involved. They have a great deal to contribute, and they are constantly looking for ways to do so. Natural leaders aren't naturally virtuous, however. Just as with designated leaders, the traits and power of the natural leader can be misdirected.

Libraries have much to gain by enlisting the talents of the natural leader and a lot to lose by squandering or opposing those talents. It is far better for everyone concerned if natural leaders can be enlisted to engage others for the good of the library.

The effective library director empowers all leaders—designated and natural. It is these people who help the director keep leadership percolating throughout the organization. Whether they mean to or not, both categories of leaders are making things better or they are making things worse according to their leadership ability.

Leaders Must Want to Work on Their Leadership

Library leaders say they use coaches for a wide range of library matters in their institutions. However, since the term *coaching* is used casually, it is difficult to know what the actual applications are. Some of these applications may indeed involve coaching, while others involve advising, counseling, tutoring, mentoring, or other forms of consulting.

Technical coaching is a type of coaching library leaders use. Examples include a library director who works with a coach to improve media relations skills, or a university librarian who hires a coach to help develop a long-term finance strategy for the library. Others avail themselves of coaching to improve their ability to effectively manage their work relationships with peers and with those who report to them or to whom they report.

Leaders generally do not talk about being coached, mainly because coaching is and should remain a privileged relationship. That is, the player is at liberty to discuss the coaching, while the coach must not. However, the fact that coaching is not something much discussed among leaders suggests that it is a tool many leaders never even consider. In hindsight, seasoned library leaders say that they would have eagerly engaged a coach had they thought it was a possibility.

One of the issues for the leader who contemplates getting a coach is how others will understand this, particularly colleagues and bosses. Some bosses will be pleased, while others might be threatened. One library board member told me the director shouldn't need a coach; at her salary, the director should know it all. Some leaders think that others will interpret the leader's having a coach or admitting to having one as a sign of the leader's inadequacy. In fact, individuals who want to develop themselves as leaders will welcome having a trusted ally whose sole purpose is to help them become the leaders they want to be.

Leaders must want to work on their leadership. They are always becoming better leaders to retain the leader's edge. The coach helps leaders understand themselves as leaders. This is a matter of leaders getting good feedback and developing awareness of what they do and why. It is a matter of leaders learning about the effect of what they do as leaders and learning through coaching and practice that there are options to take and choices to be made. Coaching leaders means that leaders become able to make conscious choices. For example:

> Charles is a leader who has earned a reputation for being impatient with staff and prone to outbursts of anger when individuals are too slow to catch on to his wishes. Charles has been cautioned about this by some of his advisers. However, he believes that his reputation with staff is actually effective in motivating them to accomplish what he wants. In fact, it does get an attentive response from some staff. However, it immobilizes some and demoralizes yet others. Coaching could help Charles realize that anger works with some people and not with others. It works in one situation and not in others.

Uncontrolled reactions or behaviors are liabilities in a leader. Effective leaders are self-modifying. That is, for the good of the library, they consciously decide to modify how they might normally react. They are able to consciously make choices that are beneficial for the library.

Leaders Need Coaching about How to Be Leaders

Coaching leaders, whether designated or natural, involves coaching an aspect of that individual. That is, the coaching is about leadership, not about the person's effectiveness as a worker, manager, or team member. Understanding this narrows the field of coaching, simplifying things for both the coach and the leader.

The substance of leadership coaching is essentially the same, whether the leader is the director or another designated or natural leader. Leaders need coaching about how to be leaders. For example, leaders must engage the commitment of those they lead with a vision, a game plan, and meaningful interaction. Leaders must know and manage their influence on others, their own strengths and weaknesses, and they must be attuned to real issues in the institution and community. The role of the coach is to help the leader who is willing to work on her leadership become the leader she wants to be.

Leaders Need a Vision

Leaders must be able to formulate, communicate, and excite others about a vision. Whether it is a vision for the whole library or a department, a project, or an initiative, the leader needs others to help this vision become reality.

Many leaders have a vision but have not verbalized it in so many words. They are undoubtedly acting on that vision, whether they mean to or not. In fact, they may *think* they have stated it or that it is apparent from what they say and do. This vision may be known to some but not to others. Staff may understand the vision, for instance, even if external stakeholders do not, or vice versa.

Some leaders don't know how to articulate their visions or don't think they have one. They are searching for a vision and looking outside themselves to discover what it should be. It doesn't occur to some that they need to share their vision or that they can marshal a vision from collaboration with others. Some leaders don't want to be held to one vision. Sometimes, what drives the leader is a vision about the leader and not about the library. Coaching helps the leader elicit a vision about the library in the context of the larger community vision.

A library vision is about creating something for the greater good. Coaching helps leaders understand they are obligated to provide a vision because people are looking for it, especially from designated leaders. When people don't see that the leader has a vision, they begin to doubt that they have a leader. Coaching helps leaders understand the importance of a vision, formulate a vision, communicate that vision, and learn how to get people excited and signed on for the quest.

Not every leader knows to do this or wants to do it. The coach helps the leader extract the vision that is often unconsciously present, dormant, unarticulated, or expressed in a way that others don't recognize as a vision. The coach is a springboard for the leader to objectively test the vision or the expression of it and to provide objective feedback about the vision to the leader. The coach helps the leader with the process of developing a vision that is big enough for everyone. For example:

> Shanice is a senior leader and collection coordinator in a large academic library. This is a position with systemwide responsibility for developing the collections and the collection policy and plan for the university system. Shanice is an imaginative, knowledgeable, and accomplished professional and a competent manager and team member. However, after a year and a half in her position, the staff are saying among themselves that they don't understand where Shanice is headed with collection development. They say that they respect her professional expertise, like her, love her ideas, and are ready to follow her anywhere. Shanice's personality and qualities obviously engage and inspire followers. However, these same people are wondering out loud about her leadership ability.
>
> Shanice's ideas are plentiful, innovative, expansive, and exciting. She thinks she has a vision, but when pressed by the coach to express it in words, Shanice recites a litany of ideas and projects she has on her mind. Her "vision" is a surround-sound of ideas and concepts bouncing off the walls. The coach helps Shanice see that these ideas and concepts, though they may fit into a vision, do not make a vision. The coach's skills, particularly inquiry and feedback, help Shanice articulate her vision. This doesn't happen necessarily in one meeting, but is a process that leads Shanice to a sense of her own vision.

Leaders Need Game Plans

Leaders at every level need a plan for reaching their vision. Call it a game plan, a road map, the yellow brick road, or whatever—without a plan, the team, the committee, the work group, the library staff, or the library stakeholders get off track.

> Once Shanice's eager followers know the destination, they are poised to help her get there. She invites their participation in the planning and enables them to influence the direction. They understand where they are going and how they will get there.

Imagine the following. You and several of your colleagues are on a wilderness experience together in the high desert country. All of you are wilderness novices. You are accompanied by two experienced instructors who will help you become conditioned for a three-day group trek. You will learn the basics—reading topographic maps, using a compass, and applying emergency first aid. The instructors will shadow the group, but the group will not see them or be in contact with them. The day arrives when the group's journey begins. The instructors take the group to its departure point and give the group its destination and the time it should arrive on the third day. They appoint you as the group's leader.

Few would argue against the importance of everyone in this group knowing the plan for accomplishing the assignment. Everyone's cooperation will be needed for the success of this trek. They must frequently refer to the map and check it against the real territory. You, the leader, will want input from the individuals in the group to help inform the decisions that invariably must be made along the way. Their feedback will help you gauge how the group is progressing. This is important because everyone's well-being is at stake.

By contrast, in real life some leaders start off without a word about the plan—just a "forward-ho" and a wave of the hand and a confident "follow me." Such leaders believe they know what is best. In essence, with no overt plan the assignment is about the leader. However, in reality, it is everyone's assignment because it takes everyone to get there, everyone has a vested interest in the outcome, and everyone's well-being is on the line. The leader who understands this is a leader with a committed and loyal following.

Smart people—and libraries are full of them—want to know what the plan is and what is expected of them; they want to have input. When people understand the plan and can see that it leads toward the vision, they are willing to get on board.

The plan doesn't have to be exact. It needs to be complete enough so the trekkers understand their role and want to make the journey. They know they can bring something to this effort, and they have a stake in its success. The plan is not a document on the shelf; it is a talked-about set of values and goals people use to get their bearings, day in and day out.

Again, the role of the coach is to help leaders understand that being a leader obligates them to provide and communicate the game plan. The leader may know the way, but what about the people on the journey? They have a stake in the outcome, and they want it to be successful. Engaging their commitment is what leaders sometimes do not know to do, do not know how to do, or do not care to do. Nevertheless, this is what it means to be a leader. No organization can perform at its best without engaging the talent of all of its players.

Leaders Create Shared Meaning

The leader understands that a high-performance library is dependent on engaging and sustaining the commitment of others to the library vision. The "others" include the library's leadership, the staff and volunteers, the library's users, leaders and policy-makers of the parent institution, and the community. Winning and sustaining the commitment to an excellent library is a 360-degree, ongoing proposition. The more engaged the stakeholders are, the higher-performing the library becomes.

Engaging individuals happens through meaningful interaction about the most important work of the organization. That is, library leaders purposefully engage the community and the staff in an ongoing dialogue about the library in the community. Establishing shared meaning is the goal of that dialogue. When people understand what the library is about, how they fit into the library's mission, and why their contribution is important, they engage.

A practical manifestation of this ongoing dialogue with the community is the library's plan. Library leaders shepherd the community into the planning process. The vision is a shared one. Another manifestation is the library's public relations program. More than press releases and brochures, public relations establishes a proactive relationship with the news media. It enables a regular dialogue with the community wherein the library asks the community how the library is doing. In turn, library leaders listen and are responsive to what the community has to say.

Inside the library, engagement is an ongoing process, too. That process includes alignment of individuals' work with the library vision, staff readiness to perform the work, and feedback about that performance. Alignment plus readiness plus feedback equals engagement. Work in the library is dynamic because it is directly related to this ongoing dialogue with the community. Library leaders steer a steady course toward the vision, but they correct course according to what they learn along the way. Goals necessarily change, thus changing the work that needs to be done. For some individuals, this is a different way of thinking about work in the library. Those who think that what they were hired to do is what they always will be doing are surprised, even resistant to this reality of dynamic work.

The library leader needs to know that establishing shared meaning inside the organization is as important as establishing it in the community, and vice versa. Often, the leader is better at engaging the commitment of one or the other of these stakeholder groups. Leaders who know their strengths and weaknesses know exactly where and how they need to compensate.

Leaders Need to Know Their Influence on Others

People in leadership positions often are not aware of how their leadership persona influences people in the organization and the community. A leader may have climbed the leadership ladder without thinking a great deal about the effect of her personal or leadership style. To her, personal and leadership style may be one and the same and simply a part of the package. This may have been a match, or at least not a clash, in those organizations for which she previously worked.

In a different organization the same leader can find herself running into trouble for the first time in her career. Her leadership style doesn't work here as it did in other organizations. Perhaps the organization is much larger and more complex or there is a different organizational or community culture. The stylistic preferences are different from what this leader naturally brings. The point is that coaching can help the leader develop awareness of her personal style. It can help her construct the leadership

persona that enables her to be more effective in her organization and the community.

People in the organization and the library community pay attention to what leaders do and say. The message from a leader can be so powerful as to become part of the institutional lore. However, the message that is received isn't always what the leader intends. The leader's feedback system confirms for the leader that her intended message has been received or that the message is confused. Thus, the leader has the opportunity to correct the message, to elaborate, and to take whatever action is necessary.

Leaders are always teaching others about themselves by how they act and by what they say. Leaders, particularly designated leaders, are perceived as powerful people. The more powerful the "teacher," the more powerfully received and lasting the message. In one instance, a library director reportedly told an assembly of staff that nothing would stand in the way of his building a state-of-the-art digital library. If people could not get on board, they should find another library more suited to their ambitions. Of course, the message morphed as it made the rounds. However, the gist of the message became part of this library's lore. What many staff heard was that this library was going places and staff could help make that happen or they could find another place to work. This piece of library lore persisted long after the director moved on. Staff who came to the library after the director had left the institution perpetuated that lore. This happens in every system. The leader needs to be aware of it and know that it can be consciously used to set up healthy lore.

Leaders Must Be Attuned to Real Issues

Real issues are often those that the library leader only knows about through other leaders in the institution or community. It is from among these leaders that library leaders get coaching on real issues. For example, an issue for the leader might have to do with fund-raising. In concept, fund-raising is a core competency these days for any library director. It would be reasonable for a library director to assume that this was expected of him. At the same time, sentiments about this vary from institution to institution and from community to community.

In one private school community, fundraising was obviously a priority. The institution had a development officer and a development campaign. However, many of the parents were philosophically opposed to the idea of the school officials soliciting benefactors. The parents did not want to be in the position of having to compromise philosophical principles to satisfy donor terms and conditions. On basic principle, they were leery of any financial dependency, be it private, corporate, or governmental. Yet they struggled to be able to afford the quality of educational program that was the very foundation of the institution.

The leader who is not attuned to such issues can make considerable trouble for the institution and the community. Coaching helps the leader understand this responsibility and home in on the real issues.

Leaders Need a Feedback System

Coaching helps leaders understand they need a feedback system. A feedback system helps leaders know how they are influencing others and what the important organizational and community issues are. How do the library's stakeholders perceive the actions of the leader? Is this what the leader intends? Is it effective for the library? For example, what is the feedback the leader gets from the speech he gave at the staff assembly? If it is what he intended, what is the receptivity of staff to his ideas and direction? If it is not what was intended, what if anything needs to be done to correct the perception?

The backbone of the leader's feedback system consists of a core group of individuals whom the leader trusts and who are loyal to the leader. These are high-functioning people who are comfortable in a free exchange of information with the leader. They are willing to stop in the leader's office or call on the telephone and vice versa. These people are connected with others in the organization through an informal network of relationships. The leader taps into this and also receives a free flow of information from the core group. This is not a formal arrangement but an organic alliance that the leader gradually develops.

A feedback system helps the leader track his influence, both positive and negative. He then makes a conscious choice about what to do about the information. The feedback system is also the leader's early warning system. An early alert to potential trouble enables him to take action to avert the trouble or to redirect it. For instance, imagine the reaction of staff when they read about a budget reduction in the newspaper before they have heard anything about it at work. The leader's feedback system conveys the effect of this message, and the leader determines precisely what he must do and the level of effort that is appropriate in this case. The leader's feedback system helps him learn about and monitor the influence of his actions.

Leaders Must Know Their Strengths and Weaknesses

Leaders need to know and acknowledge their strengths and weaknesses. By acknowledging strengths, leaders become able to consciously develop those strengths into talents. Then they become better able to consciously apply those talents at the right time and for the right reasons. Knowing and acknowledging weaknesses enables leaders to know when they are vulnerable and when to consciously control manifestation of those weaknesses and to compensate for those weaknesses.

Some strengths and weaknesses affect a leader's ability to lead others. A leader who is mentally quick may be impatient with those who are methodical and long-winded in their explanations. She may distance herself from such people without compensating in some way for what she loses by that distancing. To compensate in this case, the leader would find an alternate way to have the benefit of this person's input and perspective. She may have this person report to someone with more patience for the person's style. This someone might also be able to coach the methodical speaker toward a crisper style with this particular leader.

The point of acknowledging weaknesses is that the leader is able to know how to compensate for them. For instance, if the leader is an introvert inclined toward solitude, she needs to consciously choose to participate at times in the social life of the organization. She not only consciously chooses, but her choice of events is also consciously calculated to give her the most mileage. She relies on others in the organization to fill her in, too. The point isn't for her to become an extrovert but to consciously compensate when it is in the interests of the library for her to do so.

The leader who tends to be self-centered, has difficulty asking for help from others, or always sees the glass half empty or half full can compensate for these weaknesses. The wonderful thing about an organization is that it contains a range of strengths. The leader doesn't have to be equally talented across the full range of possibilities. She can enlist the strengths of others as well as apply hers, consciously and in the right measure, for the good of the library. Leaders learn about their strengths and weaknesses through feedback.

Who Coaches Leaders?

Generally, supervisors, mentors, and peers, both in and out of the library, coach leaders and emergent leaders. This is generally an in-kind relationship; that is, it is done on an informal basis as part of one's role in the organization. Some libraries hire coaches on an as-needed basis, while some hire coaches on an ongoing basis. For example, in one library system, a coach works with middle managers to develop their leadership ability. This both complements and supplements what their supervisors might be able to provide. Coaching is a crucial tool in developing and sustaining effective leadership, and organizational leaders who are serious about doing either should consciously make coaching available for this purpose.

People will come to coaches if they know that coaching is available to them. It takes only one or two effective coaches in the organization to seed a network of coaching, because the few players who first benefit from such coaching begin to spread the word. For example, an organizational leader might sponsor coach training for a handful of willing leaders in the library and thus create a cohort group of self-selected coaches. A library can be purposeful about launching such an effort and even focus it on a special initiative, such as leadership diversity. This coaching network need not be an out-of-pocket expense: discover your leadership coaches in the organization, and with their permission, use them.

The most compelling aspect of the question "Who coaches leaders?" is who coaches the director. Typically, someone from outside the organization coaches the director. Occasionally, the director is willing to be coached by someone in the organization. This person, of course, will be a subordinate. The issue here is that the coach from within the organization must be able to handle the differential in roles. The coach can do this by being able to shift fairly comfortably between the role of subordinate and coach. The director must trust this internal coach, as anyone else does who accepts coaching. Often, this relationship is too great a risk to the director-subordinate relationship.

The director's confidants are often other directors or they are leaders in other fields of comparable or higher status. These confidants may be within the immediate community or in the larger professional community. Library directors make these connections through associations and professional and community involvement. Usually, these are people the director has associated with over time. A level of trust has been established. Some of these peers have become confidants and friends. Still, confidentiality is an issue. Directors can't afford to have it appear that they are airing dirty laundry.

Often coaching among peers is personal rather than professional. Competition and the fact that these people are all very busy often limits how far coaching can go. It is also hard to trust someone enough to work on your leadership skills with that person. Although a director may trust a confidant, the confidant may not be able to coach the director because she may not have the basic skills to do so. Coaching is a unique relationship in which the coach and player purposefully take on the director's leadership growth. This takes the objectivity and skills of a coach.

Finding an executive coach is an option for the library director. Confidentiality is an issue. The director must carefully consider the trustworthiness of her chosen coach. The introduction to this book includes a section on finding a coach, and the "Selected Resources" list provides sources.

WHY COACH LEADERS?

If the leader isn't effective, the entire organization suffers and the community suffers. Coaching helps the leader become a better leader. He becomes more—or perhaps less—precise, focused, communicative, or whatever is needed for that leader to be effectively more powerful. The leader is always either increasing or decreasing his clout by his behavior. There is no time-out or neutral ground.

Coaching improves leadership in those who are willing to work on their leadership. Being a leader is a big job, and every leader needs the kind of help that coaching provides. This is help that makes the leader become the leader he wants to be. Leaders who aren't willing to grow and change are going to be a problem for the community, and leaders who grow establish a standard for everyone else in the organization. This makes the organization better, too.

The strengths and weaknesses of leaders are often reflected among those they lead. The team, committee, work unit, and library exhibit the characteristics of their leader. This leader-entity isomorphism is the main reason it rarely makes sense to coach a manifestation of a problem in a work group, for instance, without coaching its leader as well.

No leader, regardless of how capable, can do it all. Effective leadership must percolate throughout the organization. Coaching helps leaders know what they do well, what needs improvement, and how to improve their leadership.

HOW TO COACH LEADERS

People have or develop a leadership style based on their history and attitude about leadership and themselves. Some of the very best people—meaning "leader material"—have trouble thinking of themselves as leaders. Their understanding of what it is to be a leader clashes with how they want to think of themselves. For example, some people feel they want to be humble. However, this clashes with their image of an authoritarian leadership style, perhaps the only style they have personally experienced. Some people think of leadership as something that is too responsible, too consuming, or too domineering. This is not who they want to be; therefore, they reject the possibility of being a leader and decide they are not leadership material.

Just the notion that it is all right to talk about leadership opens the door for developing leaders. It is the first step, in fact, in developing leaders. Being willing to talk about leadership opens the topic for a healthy examination. Like parents talking with their children about sex, it doesn't much matter what they say; it is the fact that they are willing to talk about it that takes away the taboo.

Talking about leadership begins to change how people think about leadership and themselves. One way for the coach to begin this conversation with a player is to conduct a simple leadership survey. For instance, the coach might ask what the player's leadership history has been. Has she been a leader, for example, in school, an institution, or the community? What is her image of a leader? What are the characteristics she most admires about leadership? What are those she rejects? Just talking about leadership helps people begin to discover that being a leader entails a lot more than what they have experienced.

To coach a person about leadership helps her think about herself as a leader. Coaching challenges the self-image that often limits the player's concept of her leadership style and potential. For example, a person who is short in stature may have trouble thinking about herself as a leader. Gender, race, culture, education, and other issues are barriers to people's concept of themselves as leaders. Coaching helps people challenge their self-concept about leadership. It helps them discover leadership qualities in themselves that change their concept of what it means to be a leader and what they are able to do. In other words, coaching helps empower leaders.

It is possible that leadership can be a systemic issue. For instance, impotent leadership, authoritarian leadership, exclusive leadership, or other dominant characteristics of leadership in a library can be a barrier to performance and to the library's effectiveness. Likewise, diverse leadership, creative leadership, inclusive leadership, and other characteristics of the leadership system can positively influence performance and library effectiveness.

An entire organization can have issues about leadership. For instance, libraries can have their version of the glass ceiling, and people who have a certain style that is very different from the dominant style of leadership can feel that there is no real opportunity for them within the organization. If designated leaders appear to be roughly the same in terms of education, age, gender, and race, chances are this is a perceived barrier to people who work in the library or who might consider a career in libraries.

When does a coach decide that leadership should be coached? The answer is when the coach sees that ineffective leadership is hurting organizational performance. For example:

Library leaders are seriously beginning to plan for successors. They know they are facing stiff competition in the job market and that competition will increase. Many leaders believe that part of the answer is to groom at least some leaders from among those younger staff in the organization. Unfortunately, some of the best people would not even consider themselves as potential leadership successors in the manner of their library's dominant leadership style.

This is one of those situations where the right hand and the left hand are working at odds. At such times, it makes sense to coach leaders, both designated and natural, to help them become mindfully aware of this at-odds reality. Natural, undesignated leaders and potential successors can also be coached to develop their understanding of leadership and their leadership ability and style.

In this chapter's prelude, the library team was in trouble because too many of the players were on the sidelines rather than in the game. In the library leadership game, some of the best talent is on the sidelines, as is the case with Catherine. This is due, in part, to a narrow understanding of what it means to be a leader.

Catherine is a natural leader. She is also a designated leader and a middle manager in a large library system. Passionate about her work and ambitious, she is active in professional committees. There she observes and rubs shoulders with top-level library leaders. She enjoys these relationships for the intellectual and social stimulation as well as for the prestige they give her. Catherine holds these colleagues up as a stan-

dard by which to judge her leadership potential. By comparison, she believes she is different in her attitudes, approaches, and motivation and thinks these differences are liabilities. There are few other young women of color among these leaders or in her library system, and these other distinctions only make her feel that she is more out of step and that the top rung of the library ladder is out of reach. She is on the verge of concluding that she has risen as far as she can in the library profession.

In this chapter's application, Catherine's supervisor, Carlos, has been observant and mindfully aware of Catherine in the manner of a coach. Note the coaching dialogue in this application, which illustrates the coach's skill and ability and the technique of giving feedback. The purpose of the coaching is to guide Catherine toward a higher level of performance. All stages of the coaching interaction are demonstrated: initial, content, and wrap-up.

APPLICATION

SUPPORTING LEADERSHIP GROWTH

Background
In a few intensive years Catherine had worked her way up the designated leadership ladder from page to middle manager, earning a master's degree in library science in the meantime. As a child, she had drifted into her neighborhood library, where she learned she was welcomed even before she understood what a library actually was. She had not thought about becoming a librarian until years later when she had taken a temporary job helping with a library literacy program. That's when she fell in love with the idea of libraries.

While in her literacy job, Catherine realized how much she had taken the library for granted, how fortunate she had been, and how much the library could mean to those who were less fortunate. It was this realization of the meaning of libraries that impassioned her to become a librarian.

Catherine was a natural leader who advanced into increasingly responsible positions. She became involved in professional associations and their work. She was interested in changing libraries from the inside because she believed people who worked in libraries could do so much more than they were doing to make libraries accessible to the underserved. However, the entrenched pettiness, meanness, and poverty of thought that she encountered in the workplace had disillusioned her.

The designated leaders she observed disillusioned her, too. As Catherine took her own measure against what she observed of them, she could not imagine being able to force herself into the mold. She had nearly concluded that she was not leadership material in the library world and was on the verge of deciding that she must give up her library career. She doubted the efficacy of her vision of libraries for everyone.

At the same time, Catherine felt exceedingly distracted and pulled toward relocating for a period of time to the region of her ancestors to immerse herself in her writing. However, she was afraid that the library establishment would misunderstand this and that making this move would jeopardize her career. Although she was doubtful about her future in libraries, Catherine also did not want to precipitously throw away a career in which she had invested so much.

Catherine made an appointment with her supervisor, Carlos, whom she had grown to trust as a coach and adviser. She did not know exactly what to do; however, she felt she could dare to utter in Carlos's presence her unexpressed notion without fear of reprisal. She knew she could count on his honesty, his open-minded exploration of her idea, and his confidentiality.

Carlos had noticed that Catherine had become increasingly fatigued and uncharacteristically impatient with some individuals in the library. She had become pessimistic that attitudes and interactions among these individuals would ever change for the better. The intolerance and insidious bigotry seemed to overwhelm her. Her stamina in her work noticeably diminished. Carlos observed that taking time off did not restore Catherine's emotional vigor as it once had.

Three times in the last two months, Carlos had talked about his observations with Catherine. Each time, Catherine had agreed with Carlos. However, she believed that she could manage with enough effort on her part. They agreed that Catherine was doing very demanding work for the library and that there were several difficult personnel situations Catherine was managing. Catherine was also chairing the multicultural committee, which was sponsoring a dialogue in the library about diversity. This duty precipitated some demanding interactions in the library that drew in Catherine as mentor and coach and, for some, as adversary. Catherine and Carlos had agreed that these demands required setting limits to the hours Catherine worked. However, it was obvious from his daily interactions with Catherine that she was emotionally embroiled in processing off duty the interpersonal issues that arose from her work.

From time to time, Catherine mentioned aspects of her personal life that were challenging her, too. For example, she had spoken of research she was doing about her family roots. She also mentioned her journal and poetry writing, which she said was dominated by this family theme.

The Coaching Meeting

Carlos greeted Catherine with a smile as she arrived for their appointed meeting. She returned the smile but appeared heavy-hearted and weary. Carlos closed his office door, then returned to his chair as Catherine took a seat opposite him.

He caught Catherine's eye and began: "It's good to see you. Tell me, how are you doing these days and what's on your mind?"

"Well, Carlos, I'm afraid it's the same story from me again," she said with a little laugh and a hint of self-deprecation. "We've talked again and again, it seems to me, about where I am in my career and how I'm feeling about my job. I wish I could tell you that I am feeling better or more settled about both, but I cannot. I didn't come here today to try to resolve this condition I'm in. I've been over it and over it, and it just seems too hard to figure out right now. I don't know what to do, but I feel I must do something to help myself. It feels as if I'm sinking deeper into a malaise despite trying to set limits, trying to get rest, and taking little breaks from work."

Carlos paused briefly to be sure Catherine had finished her thought and then responded with this feedback. "As we've both said, your job is very demanding. You care a great deal about your work. You have some difficult personnel situations that, frankly, most other managers would simply not attempt to deal with. You challenge yourself to find a way to influence a change in some of the difficult cases under your supervision. In addition, your level of effort in coaching individuals involved in the multicultural committee is enormous. I've heard back from some of these people; they say that your influence is positively and profoundly affecting them, Catherine. They also tell me that some staff members are very upset with you; they blame you for upsetting the status quo. Can you see that this level of work you are doing is extraordinary and very, very demanding?"

(continued)

Catherine thought for a moment, then responded, "I hadn't thought about it before, really, but you've helped to put its consideration into my thinking. It's hard for me to imagine that other people in the organization don't feel about their work the way I feel about mine. I don't know any other way to be. Now that you've led me to think about it, I take time to observe from a detached point of view. I see that the work isn't so dominant with others, and there may be other things for people: their homes, their children, their art or hobbies. As for demanding, yes; I feel utterly exhausted."

Carlos asked: "What is it about your work that seems so urgent, Catherine? Why do you think that it is? We haven't really talked about what is behind your passionate attention to your work. What is your work exactly; how would you define it?"

Catherine shook her head, "Oh, dear, what a hard question." Then she sat silently and pondered for long seconds what Carlos had asked. "I haven't ever put it into words."

Catherine was silent again, and Carlos patiently waited.

Catherine realized that Carlos really wanted to know. She began, "It feels like it has to do with respect: respect in the workplace on a person-to-person level regardless of title or rank and respect from our employees toward any person of any age, race, culture, gender, or sexual orientation or intellectual or philosophic or religious belief. I want libraries to symbolize for all people that they are places of learning and of personal growth and self-development. I want libraries to be a sanctuary for this learning. I want libraries to be known by all as the places in our communities that cherish this need in people and nurture it by opening their doors wide and inviting in those least empowered. I want libraries to symbolize respect for the human condition and for human potential to rise above that which tries to keep them down."

Carlos's eyes widened. "That is a very powerful statement, Catherine, and a very compelling vision."

Carlos saw that Catherine's eyes had welled up; he silently waited. She took a deep breath and, exhaling slowly, composed herself. "And you've never heard yourself say that before?" asked Carlos.

Catherine smiled. "This is the first time. It feels good to say it and to hear it. It's freeing and settling to finally have it work its way out of me. Thank you, Carlos, for asking me. I have not even thought to ask it of myself, and it's not the sort of thing we talk about, at least not among those of us in middle management." Catherine paused and then said quietly, "How dare we have a vision, huh?"

Carlos leaned forward. "You are entitled and, indeed, fortunate to have a vision and to find it. There are leaders who need one and cannot find it or don't seek it. It's hard to be a leader without a vision. However, it's no wonder that you're fatigued! You'll have to pace yourself better than you have been doing, Catherine, if you're to survive your vision."

Catherine nodded. "I know we've talked about this before, Carlos: about setting boundaries and bringing balance into my life. I've tried to do that, but it's a real struggle. I feel compelled to fight every injustice in the workplace, and I know that's unrealistic.

"Carlos, you talk as if you think of me as a leader, but I don't feel like one. I think I will never be a library director. When I look at the ones I know, even the ones I thought I admired, I cannot see myself doing what they do."

"What is it that you see them do that you cannot see yourself doing?" Carlos asked.

Catherine responded immediately, "Well, compromising their principles. Kowtowing to the powers that be. In particular, not taking a stand on issues they were once committed to, or so I thought, before they became directors. I am amazed at the change in people I have worked alongside in professional associations, people I have admired, some who have mentored me. Now that they are directors, they have relaxed their zeal about what needs to be done in the profession and in our communities. What the people need or what staff needs in order to serve them well are the last things on their minds. Politics seem to rule them—politics and expediency. If that's what it means to become a director, I don't know that I can bring myself to it. Perhaps I'm not director material."

Carlos responded, "I don't know which people you have in mind, Catherine, and it doesn't matter for our purposes at the moment. What matters is what you make of it and how that affects your leadership self-concept.

"You know that you don't know what the whole story is with them. There's no point, really, in dwelling on it. You have much to do to create your own story, for which you and you alone are responsible. What is the merit in judging others or in being disillusioned by them? It only distracts you from your own vision and squanders your power. Why do you permit them so much influence over you, and why judge your leadership potential by what others do or don't do?"

Catherine blinked. "How else can I judge my leadership potential if not by looking at who the leaders are in the library community and evaluating myself against them?"

Carlos raised his eyebrows. "Maybe your leadership potential is not to be judged but rather to be cultivated by you being yourself and developing yourself as best you can." He paused for a response, which Catherine conveyed with a slow nod of her head.

Carlos continued, "I admit it seems logical, Catherine, to approach the notion of leadership in the way you described. However, that approach treats leadership as if it were some mathematical formula: x plus y plus z equals leadership. Some people do think of it this way, but others believe it is more organic.

"For instance, leadership always has a context: Would Gandhi have become a leader had he been born into a different era or in a different country or under different circumstances? Or were the events of his day and age and place catalysts for evoking the leader from an otherwise ordinary man?"

Catherine listened attentively to Carlos.

Continuing on, Carlos said, "Leadership is not something that someone is in the abstract, nor is it something that a person can be in isolation from other people, conditions, and events. I doubt that Rosa Parks challenged the status quo because she had thought a great deal about what it takes to be a leader or by looking elsewhere for permission to think of herself as a leader. Becoming a leader wasn't her goal.

Rather, her leadership was provoked when a bus driver insisted that she go to the back of the bus; her sense of justice was violated. No one put her into her leadership role: she stepped into leadership when she acted on her beliefs. Perhaps for you, Catherine, cultivating your vision is developing your leadership potential. Do you understand what I mean?"

Catherine thought for a moment, then she said, "It's an interesting way to think about it, and of course, it makes so much sense. Forgive me, Carlos; I feel you've just given me a gem of wisdom, and I am too tired to take it in past my ears!"

Carlos chuckled at this, and Catherine laughed too. Her mood had lightened a little.

Carlos smiled broadly. "It's all right, Catherine. You already knew the little gem of wisdom. I'm just reminding you because it seems you've temporarily forgotten it!"

Catherine smiled at the gentle teasing. Then she continued with a frown, "I'm struggling with conflicting ideas about leadership and career. I'm not sure what leadership is, and I feel dead-ended in my career."

Carlos turned serious again. "You're tired, and that's skewing your perceptions. You're a leader already. This is obvious in how others react to you—you inspire many, you are a role model for many, and you provoke those who want to maintain the status quo. You also have a successful and promising career. Yet you are unhappy. Do you know what it is you want?"

Looking up, Catherine said, "Yes, I think I do, but I'm afraid to pursue it. I don't know where it will lead or if it will help me in the end. I've put a lot of myself into building my career; it matters to me, and many of the people, despite my disillusionment, matter a great deal to me, too. If I follow my intuition, I'm also worried about how it will be understood by the library community: it may forget me or write me off for not 'paying my dues.' It's hard to think of myself as not participating—not moving and shaking in the library world. I feel as if I'll lose out, fall behind in what is happening, and be left in the dust if and when I come back."

"Where would you like to go?" Carlos asked.

Catherine hesitated, and Carlos perceived that

(continued)

she was reluctant to tell him the whole story. He continued, "If and when you come back, where will you have been?"

Catherine chuckled at Carlos's good-natured encouragement.

"You can say it out loud, Catherine, without having to do it, and I won't tell anyone, ever!" Carlos said softly.

Catherine laughed, lightened up again, and said, "I've been preoccupied with the notion of relocating, for a time, to the region where my ancestors lived. It's a crazy idea because I would have to give up so much."

Carlos asked, "What would you have to give up?"

Catherine continued nervously, "My job, for one thing; my income, for another; my apartment, my friends, my work, my ordered life—there's probably more that I'd have to give up, but those are the highlights. I know I can manage financially for a year, that I can sublet my apartment, and that my friends will not stop being friends. It's my work here and, like I said, my career aspirations that I feel are threatened by this notion."

Carlos nodded. "Let's talk about the threat. The perceived threat is that taking a year off to reflect, rest, and re-create would be misunderstood by the library establishment as somehow shirking your responsibility?"

Catherine responded, "Yes, that's what I wonder about. After all, I'd be leaving some difficult personnel issues unresolved. There's also the work with the multicultural committee—I've started working with some individuals, coaching and mentoring them. I feel I'd be abandoning them. I'm also involved in some ALA committees, and I am one of the more active members. I've made commitments into the next year."

"The personnel issues you refer to have been unresolved for years," Carlos stated. "It's only since you've come along that anyone has really tried to work with the individuals involved at the level you have. They'll benefit from that or not; it is their choosing. If you're gone for a year, they won't perish for lack of you. Another manager will take over and do only what he or she is able to do. It's not your responsibility to change these individuals before you can let them go. You understand, don't you? They're fortunate to

have had a supervisor care as you have about their development. In your absence, they may even realize that fact more than they do now.

"It's the same with the individuals you're coaching and mentoring on the multicultural committee project. No doubt they cherish you, but they've had the benefit of you. In your absence, they'll continue to grow because they've been inspired by what you've given them of yourself. Fortunately for you and them, their development is in their hands and not dependent on you. How are you doing with what I am saying?"

Catherine replied, "I'm fine. I'm hearing and listening, too. What you say is true. Please go on."

Carlos continued, "Your ALA committees will get along without you. Someone will pick up the slack. Your responsibility is to let them know your change of plans. Perhaps you can help identify someone to take your place, although you may not need to. Often, when people know why you are changing your plans, they'll pitch in and help you tie up the loose ends. I think you'll find that those you respect will respect what you're doing. Rather than diminishing you in their minds, it may raise their estimation of you.

"The library establishment includes such people, and so does this library establishment. Many people recognize the courage it takes to follow your heart. Those who think it's foolish or irresponsible—well, do you really care what they think? Furthermore, is it them or is it you who will label you 'irresponsible'? Your vision, Catherine, is about empowerment. Would you let this fear of others' disapproval hold you back? If you were advising someone you are mentoring or coaching about the very same notion, what do you think you'd be saying to her?"

Again, Catherine nodded. "You're right, Carlos. You're giving me back some perspective. This is something I want to do, and if it is meant to be, it will happen if I take one step after another to put it in place. My expectations of people have become skewed because I'm tired and discouraged. I'm the only one who can do something about that. I think that's what I perceive in myself, and I must pay attention to it."

This time it was Carlos who nodded. "I agree with you. If I may say so, it strikes me that you're fatigued, and you're also at a career crossroads. Your own wisdom is telling you to take care of the first so that you will be able to deal with the second."

Catherine clapped and said, "Carlos, that is it, exactly! You've spoken the truth when I could not find the words!"

Carlos laughed. "Yes, that's why I'm the coach, you know."

Catherine grinned, excited now at having settled part of her confusion.

Carlos continued, "Now, let's talk about this library establishment. If it's a year's leave of absence you think you want, Catherine, I would wholeheartedly support your request for it. I believe the library director will grant it, with her blessing. You've contributed a great deal to this library system, and she knows it. I expect she would be glad to have an opportunity to recognize you for it."

Catherine smiled broadly. "It's good to hear you say this, Carlos. I want to think about what you've said, but I can tell you already that I will sleep better tonight, buoyed by the thought that this dream really could happen. I feel my energy beginning to flow again, and life looks far from bleak. May I think about this and talk with you again in the next few days?"

Carlos grinned. "Of course. Until then, rest assured that I will say nothing of this to anyone. I wish you the best in contemplating this adventure. Let me ask you something else, though. Several minutes ago, when you first brought this up, the first reservation you mentioned was that you didn't know where this would lead or if it would help you in the end. Where are you with that?"

Catherine replied, "I still wonder about where it will lead, and what it's about. However, I've remembered as we've been talking that I can trust myself and depend on myself to handle whatever comes along. I wasn't born in a library, and though I love them, this adventure I'm contemplating may take me down a different road altogether. Despite my fatigue-induced lapse, I know better than to willfully insist on a course that isn't meant to be. There's nothing wrong with ambition, but I know myself well enough to realize that it's not the prize. I've never been

disappointed when I've listened to and followed my intuition. It's led me through some interesting territory, and I've always been better for it. Unfortunately, my worry demon gets the better of me when I'm tired. She's been visiting me a lot lately."

"I wish you well in your thinking about this over the next few days," Carlos said. "Whichever way it goes, we've touched on some issues that we should talk more about—but first things first. Meanwhile, if the worry demon comes again, Catherine, do bring her in to meet me. I believe we've met before, but it's always nice to see a familiar face."

Catherine rose. "I will, Carlos, believe me, I will. Thank you for your help and good wishes. I'll see you—soon—to let you know where things stand."

Coach's Reasoning

Catherine was worn out. Her job at the library was very demanding. The personnel work plus the committee work were especially challenging. Catherine also was very engaged and committed to work, and it demanded her full and complete attention. When she was not at work, Catherine was doing personal work that was also very intense and often emotionally demanding. On duty and off, Catherine was spending many hours of the day processing difficult issues. She had been doing this work for a few years after an unrelenting climb into middle management.

Catherine had also reached a career crossroads. This was a complex, long-term issue. Catherine's vision, her understanding of herself, and her expectations of herself in the world were in question. One of the ongoing issues for the coach was to wonder how much of this situation was about the institution and how much was about Catherine. Was it that Catherine had not toughened up enough? Was she picking jobs or places that were not conducive to her development? Had she actively searched out people with similar concerns to build a supportive network of cohorts? Was she able to set appropriate boundaries for herself?

The career decision is a meaty one. It would be best if Catherine treats her fatigue before

(continued)

making major decisions about her career. As Catherine rests, deals with her personal matters, and is gradually restored, she will be better able to focus on career goals.

Catherine is more interested in change than most. She needs to put her vision into words so that people can understand it. As Catherine comes to know her vision, is able to articulate it, and is able to put it out for consumption, she will be less bothered by people's pettiness. She will be too busy putting out what she believes rather than reacting to what others say.

Catherine also needs to search out people with similar, compatible interests and vision. These are people interested in change and people who have a vision. They are willing to talk about it. This will stimulate, energize, and empower Catherine rather than drain her. Her coach and advisers can suggest where she can look for this. Still, she could talk with more like-minded people as she regains her strength, should she decide to take time off. The coach can help Catherine see and acknowledge her strengths as well as areas to pay attention to as she develops.

The coach would support Catherine, should she decide to ask for a leave of absence, because he knows that she is on the verge of making a wise choice for herself. He knows there is a chance that Catherine will not return to the library; however, she deserves institutional support for her growth. She has served the library well. She is a natural leader who is likely to grow tremendously by taking the step she is contemplating. Whether for the good of this library or another employer, the institution should support Catherine's efforts.

If Catherine should decide to ask for the leave, the coach should ask her to check in with him every four months and more often if she wishes. The coach should let Catherine know that he wants to keep track of her and of how she is doing and also wants to know about her future plans as they develop. Knowing what is happening concerning Catherine's career crossroads would also help him look for a fit in the organization for this developing leader. He should make it clear to Catherine that the library leadership wants her back, but that this is secondary to supporting her growth.

Leadership, ambition, self-doubt, strengths, weaknesses, power, and authority—these are concepts not openly talked about in libraries. If libraries are to develop leaders and the leadership potential of the workforce, there must be a greater willingness to talk openly about these concepts.

6 coaching managers

IN THIS CHAPTER you will see what it means to coach the most potentially powerful group of individuals in the library—managers. How managers use their authority profoundly influences every person in the library. Managers are either making the library better or making it worse—there is no neutral ground.

PRELUDE

Jeff, a college faculty librarian, was promoted to his management position after two recruitment efforts failed to draw applicants for the vacancy. Jeff had no previous experience or training in management. However, he was experienced in the department, bright, and eager to take on this new challenge. Jeff believed that he would be an asset to management and fellow librarians alike because he understood the librarians' needs and believed he could effectively champion them at the management table.

Genise, Jeff's new supervisor, was worried that Jeff would slow her down. However, she went along with the executive decision. At the time, it seemed it was management's only alternative. She also wanted to be seen as the team player that she was.

Genise quickly discovered how little Jeff knew about management. Budgets, grant proposals, and performance issues among Jeff's staff—Jeff needed help with all of it. Genise had more important things to do than school Jeff. In the time it took to teach him, Genise concluded it was just easier to do the work herself. The best she could expect was for Jeff to handle the administrative housekeeping routines and keep a lid on trouble. If Jeff could manage that, it would be help enough in these busy times.

Genise rarely had time to talk with Jeff. Six months slipped by, and Jeff had not met with Genise more than in passing. Genise repeatedly canceled the meetings she had scheduled with Jeff because something was always coming up at the last minute. Jeff's meetings with Genise were stand-up meetings in the hall, usually brief and directive. The management meetings Jeff attended, along with his management peers, consisted mainly of instructions from Genise about deadlines and routine procedures.

The librarians who reported to Jeff respected his ability as a subject expert. However, as time passed, they found that Jeff knew little about what was going on "upstairs." They fell out of touch with management, and they worried that Jeff did not well represent the interests of the department to management.

Two years passed, followed by a budget crisis. The leadership decided to reduce management because it had grown top-heavy with deadwood over the years. Jeff's position was among those cut. Fortunately, Jeff had the right to return to his former status as faculty librarian. Genise explained to Jeff that his management position was cut because he was among the last to be hired into management. Jeff didn't believe her, however. He never really understood what Genise expected of him, but there was no doubt in his mind that in her book, and in those of the decision makers, he had failed as a manager.

What went wrong in this scenario? First, the decision makers did not plan for Jeff's successful transition to his management position; consequently, in their estimation, Jeff failed as a manager. Second, Jeff felt wronged by Genise and by the leadership because he was not given the guidance he needed. Third, the librarians in Jeff's department lost touch with management. Finally, Genise and the library's leaders were oblivious to what went wrong and their part in it.

What should have happened? As an adjunct to Jeff's promotion, a plan to help Jeff grow into his position should have simultaneously been put into place. Randy, Genise's manager, should have foreseen that Genise needed some help, too, in this transition. Randy should have acted as a coach or assigned one to facilitate this transition for both Jeff and Genise. The plan should have provided initiation and orientation for Jeff and included tutoring in the budgeting, hiring, and performance planning processes as these came into play. Furthermore, Genise and Jeff should have met periodically to track progress. Finally, with the help of a coach, Genise should have learned to convey expectations and provide feedback to Jeff in his new job.

It might seem unrealistic to suggest that the leadership should have committed scarce resources to coaching Genise and Jeff. However, such a purposeful approach would have been cost-effective in the long run because the leadership would have improved Jeff's chances of succeeding as a manager

and improved Genise's performance as well. In addition, trust would have been strengthened.

WHAT IT MEANS TO COACH MANAGERS

Potentially, managers are the most powerful group of individuals in an organization. They are in charge of budgets, hiring, resource allocation, and communication. Managers have the power to change policies, procedures, and processes and are virtually in charge of library operations.

There are powerful managers and there are powerless managers, but as the opening scenario illustrates, there are no inconsequential managers. The scenario in the prelude shows how some managers experience what it means to be a manager, that lack of formal management training, poor management modeling, and vague and inconsistent expectations from leaders cause uncertainty in the manager.

Managers often are not sure what authority and power they have. Many are not practiced in using their power and authority. This uncertainty has an immobilizing effect on managers. When managers are immobilized, they do not use their authority to influence change for the better in the organization. As the coach treats this uncertainty, the manager develops greater willingness to learn, risk, question, and act.

Managers Need Coaching about How to Be Managers

Managers need coaching to treat their uncertainty about their role in the organization. They need coaching to deal effectively with the high stress and competitiveness of the positions they hold and to help them become better coaches to others.

Across a broad spectrum of libraries, many managers are unsure of themselves. They lack confidence in their ability to satisfy leadership and staff. Many of them shrink from their important role in the organization. Managers often feel trapped in the middle, torn between staff and the leadership, and customers often have faded into the background of their concern.

Leaders are disappointed when managers don't measure up to their expectations. They may hold back from entrusting responsibilities to managers because they are not confident managers will do the job to the leaders' satisfaction. Leaders say they don't have the time to fix this condition. The result is that managers are underutilized. This reinforces the uncertainty of managers and the disappointment of leaders. There is a gap between the expectations of leadership and the capacity of managers to meet those expectations. There is also a gap between the expectations of staff and the capacity of managers to meet staff expectations. These gaps can be bridged, and coaching can help.

Today's directors and other executive leaders are focused externally more than ever before. They must be, of course. Nonetheless, this external focus is happening at the same time that our institutions are undergoing tremendous internal change. While the directors are occupied with external positioning of the library, managers are faced with internal and service transitions that are broad and profound.

Our libraries are in transition. They are "chaordic," to use a term coined by Dee Hock, founder and CEO emeritus of Visa International. He used the word *chaord* to describe any system of organization that exhibits characteristics of both chaos and order, dominated by neither.

Managers must grapple with this chaordic condition, often without the level of direction they have been accustomed to from their directors. Directors have their hands full and want more from their managers. Managers are in the vortex of the transitional whirlpool, trying to address the needs of the director, the staff, and the customer. Managers understand that the needs of the director aren't necessarily those of the staff and the needs of the staff are not necessarily those of the customer. For managers who are caught in the middle of this turbulence, coaching is a lifeline.

Clarifying the Role of the Manager

Unfortunately, many managers are still working in the manner of Genise and Jeff. Just as leaders are underutilizing managers, managers are underutilizing their subordinates. Managers are working hard, but they are not necessarily working smart. They are busy getting the work done rather than coaching others into higher levels of performance. Like Genise and Jeff, they are working within a limited understanding of what managers should be. They are doing what they think they should do, know how to do, and have grown accustomed to doing. For example:

Genise has the idea that a good manager gets the work done, no matter what. The work is to get the budget and the proposals in on time, to deal with the most pressing performance issues, and to keep the lid on trouble. Genise's primary motivation is to be seen by executive management as a team player. This underlying motivation is her standard operating principle.

Genise measures herself as a manager according to how satisfied executive management is with her. The current leadership might be relieved that she complied when they reassigned Jeff and she didn't complain. She met expectations for getting the work done, but is the leadership really satisfied with her overall performance?

It isn't that there are no powerful managers—for there most certainly are. It is that management as a whole is uneven and inconsistent. This inconsistency is accepted by many as an unavoidable reality of any organization.

Coaching helps leaders and managers have a conversation about roles and expectations. It helps leaders express their expectations in practical, realistic, and understandable terms. The coach measures the gap between these expectations and the performance of managers and helps ensure that the needs of staff and customers also are taken into account as the role of the manager is reformulated. Coaching helps gradually close the gap between expectations and performance.

The role of the manager must take into account the needs of all of the stakeholders. The primary stakeholders—those who have a stake in how effectively managers perform—are the staff, the customers, and other managers, including the director. When "good management" is too narrowly defined, it is because one of these perspectives dominates. For example:

From her director's perspective, Genise is a good manager because she gets the job done and doesn't complain. From Jeff's perspective, a good manager is one who considers the needs of his subordinates. From the staff's perspective, Jeff is a good manager if he represents well the interests of the department at the management table. For the library user, a good manager responds to the concerns of the library user.

Coaching managers involves establishing or reestablishing the library's performance standard for managers. By facilitating shared understanding of the manager's role, the coach helps develop this standard of performance. This standard represents the interests of diverse stakeholders and raises the bar of management performance. It also brings consistency to the management system and addresses the needs of all those who have a stake in the role the manager plays.

The coach works from this standard, and managers gradually understand their authority and responsibility. This shows in managers' interactions with their directors, staff, and library community. As managers uphold this standard, the customer consistently encounters capable managers who are confident of the scope of their power to act on the customer's behalf. The integrity of the management system is consistently apparent to all of the stakeholders.

Handling Competition and Stress

Some would argue that the director alone defines the standard of performance for managers: a good manager is one who accomplishes what the director needs to have that manager accomplish. The emphasis is on satisfying the leader, not on the needs of the other stakeholders and the good of the library.

This standard invariably heightens competition among managers. Those who produce according to this standard are rewarded. Others are torn between the interests of the various stakeholders. The latter group thinks, "I know this is what the director wants, but is it in the best interests of the staff or the community? How do I reconcile these competing priorities?"

Coaching brings the manager back to the library's standard of performance. According to a broader library standard, a good manager is one who balances the needs of the director, the staff, the community, and other managers. The good manager's operating principle is that the needs of all the various stakeholders are valid and important, including her own. The art of managing is being able to balance these various needs for the good of the library.

Coaching helps the manager bring her competitiveness under control and cope with the stress of being, at times, in the middle of conflicting needs. Coaching helps the distraught manager settle down so that she can attend to others and to the library. Through coaching, the manager finds the narrow pathways through the thicket of competing needs. This is the art of managing.

Focusing on the Most Important Work

The purpose of coaching managers is to empower them for the good of the library. Empowered managers gradually focus their attention and energy on the right work. They are able to effectively focus resources on achieving the library vision, and they change for the better what they and only they can do—bridging the gap between the vision and the reality of where the library is headed. They do this through meaningful interaction with the leadership, individuals, and teams. Managers integrate the vision and translate that vision to others throughout the organization. They are translators, interpreters, and guides for others. They turn vision into reality.

Managers focus the resources of the organization on achieving the vision. This means that they translate the vision into goals. The goals focus the work of individuals and teams. When managers have meaningful interactions with individuals and teams about the important work of the library, they engage these people in aligning their work with the goals. Managers coach others into ever more effective ways of being in the workplace: interacting, creating, processing, and producing.

The coach helps managers put aside the work they are used to doing or prefer to do if it is not the work the organization needs from them. For instance:

> Genise is busy with the immediate and the expedient. She is willing to spend her time doing work her direct report should be doing. This is not the best use of Genise's time. Her manager, Randy, should be asking for more than this from her.

There is a trickle-down effect when managers are underutilized. The source of this is generally at the senior manager level of the organization. Genise is an example.

> Genise does some of Jeff's work and no doubt Randy does some of Genise's work, too. Randy doesn't understand why Genise can't rise to the occasion. He doesn't know how to talk to her about what he expects and needs from her.

Managing only in the "Genise" model is shortsighted and ultimately harmful to the library. The unfortunate result is that everyone is working below her or his capacity.

To turn this around, senior-level managers have to be willing to work on changing how they manage. Some think they do not have the time to communicate what they need and want, but they must make the time. This is a matter of reordering priorities. Making the time is what managers often need coaching about. Making the time for the right work and doing some of this work is harder than doing business as usual. What is the "right work" of a manager? It involves leading, finding common ground, coaching and giving feedback, and changing the library for the better.

Leading

One aspect of the manager's job, of course, is leadership. Few would quarrel with this statement in the abstract. But what does leadership from a manager look like in day-to-day practice?

Managers turn vision into reality. Managers can become trapped in vision limbo. On the one hand, they are responsible for setting work expectations and performance goals. On the other hand, they feel they lack the context for doing this, perhaps because there is no library plan, or it is dated, or it is gathering dust on a shelf in the office.

Of course, managers can be far more effective when they understand and are able to speak authoritatively about where the organization is headed. The problem often is that managers, even senior managers, may feel as if they do not know enough about where the organization is headed to speak authoritatively about it. Everyone is looking up the chain of command for vision, direction, and permission.

To coach managers is to help them establish a visionary basis for framing the practical work of those who report to them. Even in the absence of a clear understanding from the top about where the organization is headed, the manager can find visionary evidence in the organization. This evidence can be gleaned from conversations with leaders, dusty plans, conversations with the staff of the library, and community conversations. To coach managers is to help them learn to influence and help shape a vision for those they lead and to set a course for those they manage. As the following example shows, coaching managers means encouraging them to chart a course on visionary evidence, rather than waiting to be sure that what they do is okay with everyone.

For Shanice, the collections coordinator, this means providing a vision for the development of the collection. This vision emanates from the larger vision or visionary evidence of the library. Shanice and her team develop goals and strategies that provide a frame of reference to those who actually build, maintain, and manage the collection. They use this frame of reference to make decisions, both long-term and short-term, about issues such as the following.

- If we spend this much money annually on collections, how shall we focus that spending?
- We cannot buy everything we want and need. So what will be the basis on which we make decisions about spending limited resources?
- What will be the basis in the face of rising subscription costs with a static budget?
- How will we allocate additional funding for collections?

The frame of reference Shanice provides enables others to answer such questions and focus their work.

Coaching helps Shanice understand and develop this leadership capacity. Shanice is advising and influencing senior leaders who are counting on her expertise. Shanice is conveying her vision and is influencing and being informed by those who report to her. This informed give-and-take helps Shanice and those who report to her find common ground for making day-to-day decisions. They can proceed with meaningful work in the framework that Shanice has provided. She helps influence and flesh out the library vision. The senior leaders, Shanice, and those who report to her are all working within the same context. This is Shanice doing the right work.

Finding Common Ground

Managers need to be able to collaborate, negotiate, and build consensus among those who report to them and among themselves. The director cannot be in the position of arbitrating manager competition; therefore, managers need to be able to work together. They work with basic ground rules and the assumption that it is their responsibility to work together. They use organizational points of reference such as library plans and other grounding documents.

When people complain that communication is problematic in organizations, what they often mean is that understanding is lacking. That is, a shared vision and common ground are lacking. The coach develops managers beyond the messenger role into the role of facilitating understanding, a much more active role for the manager. Managers accomplish this by acquiring an understanding of what others in the organization believe, think, and want. By synthesizing this information, they are best positioned to contribute solutions and to help others in the organization continually reestablish common ground.

For example, if you were in the role of mediating a dispute between two neighbors, you would have to hear and understand what they both believed happened and what they wanted. This information enables you to see how harmony might be restored when the neighbors cannot see it. They do not have the understanding that you do because they do not have the information you have. The communication role of the manager is not as messenger but as synthesizer, mediator, consensus builder, and reconciler. The manager is constantly helping reestablish organizational equilibrium and refinding common ground among people.

The most important work of a manager is to focus individuals and teams on their most important work and to facilitate the accomplishment of goals that will move the organization toward its vision. There is always more to be done in any organization than can possibly be done. What moves the organization forward is the strategic focusing of resources on that which is most important to accomplish. People are motivated to accomplish goals when they understand why the goals are important. Facilitating this understanding is one of the most important functions of a manager.

Coaching and Giving Feedback

Managers are the most likely people in the organization to coach staff and each other. As managers learn to coach, they are better able to focus others and one another on the most important work of the library. This clarifies expectations and establishes boundaries that people need when they work. Boundaries enable individual accountability. Most people are willing to be accountable when they know their responsibilities. It is when people do not know what is expected of them that they fall into doing less important work.

As people learn what is expected and receive regular, specific feedback, they become more comfortable with the idea of taking responsibility. Without specific feedback, people tend to believe that criticism is personal and irrational. They think, for example, "The boss is just being difficult. He's having a bad day and taking it out on me." This doesn't have to happen too often for people to feel there is irrationality to all authority. They become defensive instead of learning what will enable them to do a better job.

As managers learn to coach, they become more adept at giving feedback to individuals and teams. Effective feedback helps individuals, teams, and other managers make the appropriate course corrections. It acknowledges their work and recognizes their accomplishments. Regular, specific feedback strengthens accountability. The manager begins to see consistent follow-through. With good coaching from the manager, individuals and teams become more willing to take responsibility.

Changing the Library for the Better

Managers are positioned to profoundly influence the overall effectiveness of the library. There is little that they collectively cannot change for the better if they are so minded. This means, however, that managers use their power for the good of the library. They work collaboratively, balancing the interests of all of the stakeholders. Together, they discover what must be their most important work in their organization and focus resources on it, even as they scramble to handle the mundane. They sustain that important work even when others cannot see its importance. They mindfully, consciously make decisions and choices.

Library directors need managers to lead change for the better, and library directors want to be briefed about solutions that managers are poised to implement. Directors want to have confidence that their managers have looked objectively at the span of possible options and weighed them as the leaders themselves might have done. Directors want managers to recommend the remedy that is the best, all things considered, and to know that managers understand possible consequences and are ready to deal effectively with them. Directors want managers to have thought through all the moves on the chessboard before briefing them. Then these directors may be able to add value to the deliberation. Effective leaders want their managers to take it this far.

WHY COACH MANAGERS?

You coach managers because they are in a position to influence the effectiveness of others. If managers are not improving the effectiveness of others, they are detracting from the effectiveness of the library. Managers are the most likely people in the organization to coach. However, this doesn't mean they *will* coach or that they will coach *well*. It makes sense to coach managers to make them better coaches.

Coaching managers helps them learn how to calm themselves. Managers become unsettled primarily because they are in the middle, which is stressful and competitive. The middle is full of competing needs and demands. Managers worry that they may lose face and that they might not be up to the job. They worry about being out of favor with the boss, the staff, or both. They worry about having to make decisions that might work for the short term but that they fear will be harmful in the long term.

Being a manager is a competitive job. The manager is competing for personnel, resources, and recognition from stakeholders. Coaching managers helps them learn how to bring their competitiveness under their conscious control. When managers are competing, they are not at their best. The competitiveness has to be calmed before the manager can help others.

HOW TO COACH MANAGERS

To coach managers means the coach must appreciate and deal with the conflict that goes with being in the middle. The middle is full of contradictions about what is in the best interests of the library. Managers constantly have to balance themselves in this middle. For example, if the director defines what is in the best interests of the library one way and the staff defines it another way, the manager can feel caught in a conundrum.

Coaching managers also helps them learn that their responsibility to the library is the fulcrum of that balancing act. This is what managers must come back to again and again. The side issues and competing agendas often obscure the essential issue. To coach managers is to help them learn to make the distinction between essential and side issues. Managers with the skill to differentiate these issues are poised to focus the stakeholders on what is in the best interests of the library. This is common ground. Repeatedly finding common ground is the art of being in the middle.

Coaching managers helps them learn that there are generally ways to address the side issues and competing agendas without compromising the essential solution. It is the manager's role to help address the side issues, too. To coach managers is to help them see themselves in this role and to help them cultivate the characteristics that make them able to solve problems. These characteristics include insight, resourcefulness, patience, and self-confidence.

Managers question what actually is in the best interests of the library. For example, if staff want to see an internal candidate promoted, is it in the library's best interest to comply? After all, wouldn't this send an important message to staff that management values them? However, if the director wants a manager to hire the best possible librarians, should the manager's loyalties be with the staff or with the director? Taking one position will make the manager lose face with the other.

This chapter's application illustrates the power managers have to make things better or worse. It also is an example of managers finding the narrow pathway through the seeming conundrum of workplace situations. In the application, two managers feel pressured to promote an internal candidate who has been clearly outperformed in interviews. They don't want to lose face with the director, the internal candidate, or staff who have been pressuring the managers for weeks. Note how a coach challenges them to find a solution that does not compromise the process or their responsibility to the library.

In the coaching interaction in the application, three coaching techniques come into play:

- process coaching
- coaching intervention
- confronting

Process coaching is a technique for developing higher levels of performance in individuals and teams. A coaching intervention is an interruption by the coach to influence the course of events. Confronting occurs when the coach calls the player's attention to an aspect of the player's performance. In this case, all three techniques are used in a team setting. The coaching intervention is used with the team and with the two managers who are on the team. Both the managers and the team are confronted by the coach about their performance.

Process coaching takes place while a process is under way. The coach pays particular attention to the process and coaches the team relative to it. The goal is to ensure process integrity. For instance, process coaching is used in a personnel-selection process in the following application. The coach sees the process through with the team by observing, providing feedback, and if necessary, confronting the team or individuals on the team.

APPLICATION

FOCUSING ON PERFORMANCE AND PROCESS

A cross-functional team was assembled to evaluate candidates for six librarian positions. The team consisted of several support staff, librarians, supervisors, and two managers. Among the candidates was an internal applicant. The team was responsible for evaluating and ranking in priority order the top six finalists from a dozen semifinalists. The hiring manager delegated candidate selection to the team and was not present for the candidate interviews or for the team deliberations; however, he would be the one to offer top candidates the positions. A process coach was assigned to the project to observe and coach the process while the selection team evaluated and recommended those who should be offered the positions. Being part of a hiring process like this was a first for several of the team members.

In addition to hiring the best candidates, the hiring manager also wanted to test the viability and efficiency of the team approach to selection. He wanted to be able to trust that this process could be delegated to a team without compromising the goal of hiring the best staff.

The process coach looked at how line staff were prepped for the process. She observed how the team handled communication with staff about the positions being filled and noted how individuals from different levels of the library treated conflict and authority in a team-based selection process. The coach observed these staff as they were learning firsthand how the selection process actually works. With these multiple agendas, the coach monitored the integrity of the process itself.

Observation

The team advanced an in-house candidate through the final stages of the selection process. In the final round of interviews, other contenders appeared to outperform this in-house candidate. Some of the team members questioned the in-house candidate's advancement, but the managers dismissed their concerns. This dismissal caused the coach to finally intervene. Once she did, calling the team's attention to this, some individuals acknowledged that they had observed this dismissal of concerns, too. They said they did not protest because they thought the managers and more experienced members of the team would have said something if necessary. Meanwhile, the managers insisted that the candidate in question had excelled even though the scores and notations of the team as they were reread around the table indicated otherwise.

As members of the team began to elaborate on their concerns about the candidate, the two managers held to their position. However, the comments of the team members could no longer be refuted. The managers finally disclosed what was motivating their irrational denial of their teammates' concerns: "Employees will be watching to see the organization demonstrate a commitment to a candidate who has worked her way up in the organization."

In a coaching intervention, the coach intervenes at a crucial juncture. In this case, the coach was disturbed by the managers' behavior with the rest of the team. She also wanted to further investigate their alleged reason for behaving as they had.

> Between candidate interviews, the coach caucused with the managers. She confronted the managers with her observation. They seemed to be running a different play than the rest of the team. She asked what was going on.
>
> In the privacy of the coaching intervention, the managers admitted to the coach that they were afraid of losing face. One said, "I'm worried about what longtime employees will think of us and how we will be treated if we fail to secure one of these jobs for the internal candidate. For weeks now we have been lobbied on the candidate's behalf. What will that candidate think of us if she isn't chosen? We have worked many years together, and she has gone to bat for us a few times. We owe her, don't we?"

Diagnosis

The managers on the team had advanced the candidate, in part, out of self-interest. They had not disclosed their motives to the team: they wanted the approval of the staff for themselves and for management overall. They knew staff wanted to know that the organization valued its own.

In operating as they did, the managers cut the process short and shortchanged the team and the candidate. Had these managers been acting in good faith, they would have disclosed their motives to the rest of the team and trusted the team to deal with them. They would have encouraged the team to address the interview-performance concerns directly with the candidate. This would have given the candidate an opportunity to redeem her ratings with the evaluators. The individuals who spoke up and then backed off, the managers who dismissed the other team members' concerns, and those other team members who silently colluded in the dismissal of the concerns their teammates raised jeopardized the integrity of the process. In so doing, they made the library vulnerable to formal, even legal challenge. All had put self-interest ahead of their responsibility to the team, the candidate, and the library.

The managers had falsely concluded that their needs and those of the library were ir-reconcilable. They prematurely jumped to a solution that would serve their interests. They had not trusted the team to find a solution that would address their dilemma while maintaining the integrity of the process. This was not operating in good faith with the candidate or the team. Had they been fair with the in-house candidate and other candidates, they would have found a way to follow up on the interview assessment. The managers had settled on a solution to the problem and short-circuited the process that could have worked for them, too.

Prognosis

The course the managers had chosen by insisting that the candidate outperformed other candidates would ensure the in-house candidate an offer of a position. It would thus have served the team's immediate purpose. The managers would stand in good stead with those who had been lobbying for the internal candidate, and this sense of obligation to the candidate would be satisfied.

However, proceeding in this way would have harmful long-term consequences for everyone concerned and for the library. First, it would not clear up the doubt that other team members had about the candidate. Second, it would have negative consequences for the relationships among the team members and between staff and management. Third, it would undermine the credibility of the team-based selection process. Finally, it would short-circuit further inquiry with this candidate about her interview performance because the in-house candidate would not get useful feedback from the team about her interview. Furthermore, team members could formally or informally challenge the process because their comments to others about the process could find their way to other candidates who could justifiably challenge the process. This could have legal and financial consequences for the hiring manager, the library, and its parent organization.

Now that the issue was out in the open, the team and the managers would no longer be able to deny the discrepancy. The team, candidate, and managers all would lose out in this process, or the team would come together to sort out this tangled web.

(continued)

Treatment

The coach knew that first, the team must resolve the recommendation concerning this candidate, and they must do so without violating the integrity of the process. Several team members had had concerns about the candidate, and when the managers overrode their concerns, these team members withheld their follow-up questions. They felt that these questions might have clarified their uncertainty, one way or the other. For the candidate's sake, the team would have to find a way to remedy the team's uncertainty about the candidate.

Additionally, the team must reconcile the breach of faith instigated by the managers. Regardless of the decision about the in-house candidate, the whole team had some fences to mend. The managers had overstepped their authority to influence the team and had discounted those who had tried to express their concern. They had broken faith with the team by putting self-interest ahead of the team and the library. Other team members had allowed the process to go forward, too. They sat silently by in spite of their misgivings while their teammates' concerns were brushed aside. For everyone's sake, this team had to reconcile what occurred within the team.

Finally, the managers had to acknowledge that their agenda interrupted and jeopardized the process for all concerned. The managers' face-saving concerns were understandable. However, their decision to act on those concerns in the way that they did was a misuse of their implied authority. The managers owed the team an explanation and an apology. This would help the team understand why the managers behaved with the team as they had.

The coach confronted the whole team because the team had sat silently by as the managers advanced their candidate. Several members of the team had noticed the discrepancy, but the managers had downplayed it, and this had silenced the other members of the team.

This confrontation with the team is like half-time in the locker room. The coach confronts and then refocuses the team on the ultimate goal of the process.

The team had allowed a couple of their elite players to grandstand. Now they realized this might cost them the game. The face-off in the locker room made the managers come clean about their motives.

The team opted to have a follow-up session with each of the top candidates, which all agreed included the candidate in question. They spoke with each candidate specifically about his or her strengths and discussed outstanding issues the previous interviews had left unresolved. This allowed the team to give feedback to the candidates as well as to clarify concerns. The team also restored the integrity of the process by providing all of the final candidates the same opportunity to address issues that were still in doubt. As a result, the team was able to reach consensus on the ranking of its final candidates.

The team based their recommended ranking on an honest evaluation of each candidate's suitability for the job. Once they honestly sorted through the mixed feelings and side issues, they were able to zero in on what was really relevant. Without discounting these other issues, the team could see now that it had gotten sidetracked.

The team reconciled the breach of faith. The managers acknowledged that they had thoughtlessly broken faith with the team. They explained that they had begun the process convinced that their candidate was qualified. They had focused on evaluating the other candidates, never entertaining the notion that the in-house candidate might not be a top-ranking finalist. When her selection was challenged, the managers said that they had panicked because all they could think of was what staff would think of them if they were not powerful enough to secure the candidate's selection. They had not thought to confide their predicament to the team.

Other team members admitted that they had deferred to the higher-ranking managers. They, too, had entered the process understanding that they were to be equal partners in the selection process. Yet they had doubted themselves when the managers had invalidated their observations. Some admitted having held back when they should have acknowledged their teammates' concerns.

The two managers acknowledged that their self-interest had nearly derailed the process. They realized that this would have been unfair to the candidates, team, hiring manager, and library. They realized now that their actions might have had legal and financial consequences for individuals, library, and the parent institution. They were able to see that they had nearly abrogated their responsibility as managers. They could see now that their personal agenda was driven by their need to appear powerful to staff and the in-house candidate. On reflection, they realized that this neediness made them vulnerable rather than powerful. When they thought about it, they also realized that the in-house candidate would want to be selected on her merits, not as a favor or out of a false sense of loyalty.

Ironically, the in-house candidate withdrew her candidacy for personal reasons, although she was among the top-ranked candidates. This final turn of events was one more important lesson for the team and for the managers: stay on task, trust the process, and let things take their course.

People getting sidetracked with personal agendas and acting on their own behalf is not unusual. Unfortunately, this happens frequently enough in organizations that it has far-reaching consequences for the library's effectiveness. These types of occurrences contribute to broad-based mistrust within an organization, which undermines the performance of individuals and teams and the overall effectiveness of the library.

What is unusual in this case is that there was someone paying attention to the process. Of course, it is unreasonable to think that every process will have a coach. However, it is reasonable to expect individuals, teams, leaders, and managers to be mindfully aware of what is in the best interests of the library. With coaching, the goal of the process was realized, and the players learned a great deal about their responsibility in such a process.

7 coaching & organizational effectiveness

ONE OF THE purposes of this book has been to develop the reader's sensitivity to conditions that threaten the effectiveness of the whole library. The previous chapter's application was an example of how those broad-based conditions are fed. This chapter is about how coaching addresses these conditions and improves the whole library.

PRELUDE

Just a few days away from the reopening of the renovated library, Patti, the manager, calmly confided that things felt out of control. Surprisingly and curiously, she thought, she was feeling okay about that. "There are so many people making this library reopening and community celebration happen," she said. "Dozens of people throughout the system are working on this. I know it will all come together. If there are glitches, these people care enough to make it work. I trust them. I feel like I should worry, but I know I don't have to."

How do you know when an organization is effective? You know an organization is effective when things get done well and easily, people work easily together, and processes work easily. Individuals and groups of people are able to get work launched and get great results without getting bogged down in interpersonal conflict or in process. Self-confidence, tolerance, celebration, and good-natured humor dominate the atmosphere. New processes emerge as they are needed. People understand that their jobs are more than completing tasks and that success for the customer means that staff work together for the good of the whole library's community. In organizations like these, people learn that they can handle whatever comes along.

Staff and management work toward the same ends in an effective organization. Individuals know their parts to play in reaching shared goals and vision. They are mindfully engaged in using and developing their talents for the good of the whole. People are not fussing over themselves and among themselves, because they have more important things to do. They are clear and confident about what they contribute and assume that others are contributing their best. Their focus is outward on the customer and on providing services that will continually satisfy the needs of their community.

An effective organization has vitality. Because the important work is about the customers and making wonderful services happen for them, the library—academic, school, public, or special—is perceived as a credible, generative institution within its community. Individuals are proud to be associated with the library, and those who are not associated with it would like to be. There is a sense of community pride about the library and among those associated with the library—staff, volunteers, board members, benefactors, and beneficiaries. Its many fans are cheering for the library!

As an organization becomes more effective, there is less "ado" about nothing. Instead of feeling as if they are working hard and never getting enough done, people who work for an effective organization find that they have less to do and are accomplishing a great deal. The organization works more easily than it has in the past. Something is easier this year than last. Change and the challenges that go with change are normal and all in a day's work and are taken in stride more than in the past.

An organization that integrates coaching into its day-to-day routines becomes profoundly affected. Just as a commitment to coaching over time becomes apparent, so too does the absence of it. You can tell whether you are in such a place by simply listening and observing.

The following scenarios illustrate this contrast. In the first scenario, imagine you are hearing the internal dialogue of Gabrielle's coworker as she begins a workday in the library. In the second scenario, imagine you are hearing the internal dialogue of Abdul's coworker from the library in a different city.

Scenario 1

I am a reasonably generous and fun person in my world outside of work, but when I come to work, I feel like I have to be different, more guarded and closed down. I don't actually like myself as much because of what I'm thinking and the way I act. For instance, first thing this morning when I saw my supervisor come into the area I thought how rarely she does that. Usually it means something is wrong, someone has done something they shouldn't have, or she needs

something—usually right away. Otherwise, she usually doesn't speak to me; it's like I'm not there.

At lunchtime, I ran into the new person, Gabrielle. She had a lot of questions. I remember that when I first came to the library I had a lot of questions, too. I had to figure out most things on my own. When I asked questions of a couple of people, I must admit, I was pretty grateful to them for helping me out. Too bad that they have left the library since then.

Gabrielle's already asking about other jobs in the library. She saw the posting in the staff room for library assistant. She hasn't been working here very long and she's already looking to advance. She'll find out soon enough that managers here don't think well of that. The policy is "no transfers or promotions until you have been in a position for at least a year." I'm not sure why. It's not as if they invest a lot in a person's training.

I'm getting up the courage to apply for that job myself. I've been passed over for library assistant twice already, so maybe there's probably no point in my applying. I don't really know why I was passed over. When I asked, the HR person was pretty elusive. He said I was just up against some stiff competition. Still, I'd like to know what I could do to improve. I think the best advice I can give Gabrielle is that she stay in her current job a while.

Scenario 2

Boy, I'm tired this morning. I am looking forward to my workday, though. I'm helping to orient a new guy, Abdul. He'll be shadowing others and me in the workroom for part of the day. It was fun working with the team of clerks to develop the orientation and training program for the new clerks in the system. The skit about our organizational culture that the work group did was hilarious. I've never seen my supervisor laugh so hard—especially at the part about him! I learned a lot, too, from working with the other clerks and from the skit—the follow-up discussion was really helpful.

I'm having lunch with a couple of the library assistants who are going to talk with me about what it's like to be a library assistant and what they thought helped them in their interviews. I've applied a couple of times already. I've been impressed by the other applicants. The interviews actually put us together for part of the time. I have to admit these other applicants really are good. I can see that it's a hard choice when you're filling only one or two positions.

By going through the process, I've learned a lot about what is expected of the library assistant and about the library and how it is changing. I learned a lot about myself, too. I scored higher the second time around, and I know it's because I went through the process and got a lot of help from people, including the competition! Both times, the hiring managers have offered to give applicants feedback about their examinations. I wasn't going to do that, but some coworkers and my supervisor encouraged me. So I did.

Each of the two hiring managers gave me specific feedback about how I did. Now I know that the next time I interview, I need to say more about myself. I had assumed that because I work here the interview panel knew what I'd accomplished. It's a little intimidating to go into a room with bigwigs who are going to judge me. My coworkers and my supervisor encouraged me to remember that interviewers aren't all managers and that everyone there has been through the same kind of thing.

The interviewers did seem pretty humane and interested in me. I also realized from the reference desk part of the exam that I need practice using the electronic resources under pressure while customers are waiting. My work team, supervisor, and I made a plan that freed up twelve hours over the next month so I can train at different information desks—the slow, the medium, and the really busy.

Openly talking about the promotional process takes the mystery and most of the fear out of it. I've gotten great feedback and support from coworkers, my supervisor, and the managers in the library. It's pretty obvious that people here care about my success. I want to be able to do that for others, too.

The first scenario projects a sense of workplace isolation, guardedness, and scarcity. The person has to think twice about helping a coworker. The coworker's advice to Gabrielle will be cautious and conservative, if not self-serving. You can surmise that in the second scenario there is a free flow of information and a willingness—even eagerness—to support people in their growth. The worker in the second scenario is open to learning, growing, and supporting others, too.

An effective library organization easily handles what other organizations find difficult or impossible. Its readiness is so transparent that the observer simply takes it for granted. This transparent readiness underlies the organizational ability to perform exceptionally well. As with a highly performing athletic team, the staff's ability to achieve this state of ease takes purposeful, disciplined, and sustained conditioning. The professional sports team makes its sport look easy, but the performance has taken years of conditioning that was guided and aided by coaching.

WHAT IT MEANS TO COACH FOR ORGANIZATIONAL EFFECTIVENESS

By helping individual and team performance, coaching can improve *organizational* effectiveness. As individuals and teams, leaders and managers improve their effectiveness, the overall effectiveness of the library improves, too.

However, the performance of individuals and teams in general can be capped by conditions within the organization. Low morale, negativity, lack of trust, aversion to risk, and other conditions are symptomatic of an organization that is not functioning at its best. When conditions such as these are widespread, it is vital to understand and to treat the causes. As these are addressed, the cap on individual and team performance lifts.

To coach for organizational effectiveness means to also address organizational conditions that impede individual and team performance. For example, the coach in the following scenario has undermined the effectiveness of her high school basketball team. She made winning this season her priority and in the process lost the respect and trust of the team.

The team has the best talent, woman for woman, of any team in the league. These players love their sport, and they love to play as a team. They are disciplined about staying in condition and practicing. They care about the team, and they want to win.

However, the coach tends to favor one player. This player skips practices, is out of condition, and talks back to the coach. She grandstands in the games. She monopolizes the ball and the shots. Though the coach doesn't approve, she can't bring herself to discipline this player. The coach starts this player in every game and plays her more than any of the others. This player is a good athlete, and she scores a lot of points that have won a lot of games.

The coach's behavior has caused a serious morale problem for the team. A winning team takes more than a few talented individuals. Success depends on how well all of those talents are managed. It depends on the players being well prepared and motivated, morale being good, and the array of technical and strategic decisions being soundly made. In the preceding example, self-interest and short-term gain eventually led to a problem throughout the team. Under these conditions, no matter how talented or disciplined the individual team members are, they will not be able to perform at their best.

Low morale, negativity, immobilization, intolerance, and other such characteristics of an organization have to be addressed on a large scale. These types of systemic conditions are not easily corrected not only because they are broad-based and imbedded. They also seem normal to the people who have lived with the conditions for some time. These conditions usually are created little by little. The high school coach can be fired and a new coach brought in, but the former coach's effect on the team remains and must be treated by the new coach.

Leaders are often unaware of how profoundly the organization is affected by what they routinely do or don't do. For example, leaders need people in the organization to be creative and to take risks. However, the same leaders may overreact when staff initiative goes awry. Leaders need staff to be committed to the library; however, they may fail to engage staff in meaningful interaction about the important work of the library. Leaders need accountability in their libraries, but they may overlook rather than confront behavior that is ineffective. Leaders want productive, effective organizations, yet they may do little to enable people to improve their performance.

To coach for organizational effectiveness means to be mindful of these inconsistencies and to act purposefully to correct them. Leaders and managers, in particular, must routinely ask themselves if what they do, day in and day out, is conditioning the team for its best performance. Are leaders and managers coaching the team for the long haul as well as watching today's scoreboard? Their decisions, actions, and behaviors today create the organizations they and their successors manage tomorrow.

Coaching for organizational effectiveness means developing the organization dynamically. The world is changing, our communities' needs are changing, and technology is constantly changing what we can do and how we can do it. The issue is: are we able to change nimbly to adjust to the changing times?

Many library leaders are worried about managing this. They find that they and their executive and management teams do not know how to go about structuring and successfully implementing what libraries urgently need: the evolution of twenty-first-century service, organizational, and funding models. The ability to effectively tackle such institutional challenges is fundamental to the success of leaders and the survival of libraries.

Library organizations need a culture of coaching. That is, a coaching mindset and behaviors inculcated throughout the organization. Not a single coach but many coach-minded, coachable people mindfully observing the development and the effectiveness of the organization. Integrating coaching into a library organization enables that institution to successfully adapt to the changes it faces.

Assessing Organizational Well-Being

How do you gauge the well-being of your organization? The organizational milieu is full of signs of the organizational condition; the coach develops sensitivity to this. The coach's work involves monitoring the condition and fitness of the organization. In their individual and team coaching situations, coaches often see signs of systemic performance barriers such as those described in figure 1.1 That is, they begin to see patterns of thought and behavior, to hear themes that tell them about the organization.

Meetings, for example, are windows into the organization. They reveal a great deal about an organization's efficiency and productivity as well as about how individuals interact with one another, how well a group of individuals is able to produce results, and what blocks or facilitates their success. The coach listens to what people in the organization say about themselves, each other, the library, and the organization, as well as listening for what they don't say.

Often the presenting problem is a symptom of a larger problem. The coach treats the presenting problem but also mindfully traces the symptoms to the root cause or causes, which also must be understood and treated. For example:

Anita was working with a group of managers over several months, helping them through a budget transition. The managers were dubious about getting buy-in from their staff to the changes they were proposing. They felt they didn't carry much weight with staff. Over the course of this work, all of the managers at one time or another had made reference to an employee, Brad, and his tendency to berate and bully others. All of them had firsthand knowledge of this behavior because they had witnessed it, including having been at one time or another on the receiving end. Even though Brad and his behavior was not the subject of the meetings, these managers were clearly preoccupied with Brad, recounting their experiences with him when they came together.

One day in a meeting with all of them, the subject came up again because there had just been another incident. Anita put aside the immediate work of the managers and asked the group if anyone in the organization had ever confronted Brad about his behavior. The managers all looked knowingly at one another and then at Anita but said nothing. As Anita pressed them about this, the managers told her that Brad was a union leader and influential with the library's leadership. They said they wouldn't dare confront Brad for fear of being undermined by the library's leadership.

This exchange was a window into the organization. It gave Anita information that eventually had relevance in numerous individual coaching interactions at all levels of the organization. Its immediate relevance, however, was for coaching the managers who were intimidated by Brad's power.

The managers were letting fear keep them from doing their jobs. An organization cannot be fully effective when managers are afraid to do their jobs. It cannot be effective when individual performance is governed by a few strong personalities in the organization, and it cannot be effective when managers and staff collude in perpetuating dysfunction out of self-interest.

If the managers were afraid to tackle this problem, what else would they let slide? How had it affected the organization? How could they use their authority more efficiently and productively? From the taxpayer's point of view, what value is added by the presence of these managers if they are afraid to manage?

Anita knew that the managers' behavior was far more troubling than Brad's behavior. Not only were the managers ineffective with Brad, but they were generally ineffective as leaders of staff. The managers also did not protect staff from Brad's bullying. When it came to aligning with power, the staff knew there was no con-

test: Brad was their man. Anita thought it no surprise that these managers lacked credibility with staff.

Anita was able to learn over the long term how other behavior in the organization reinforced the behaviors of these managers and of staff. For instance, higher-level managers colluded with Brad. They could find out from Brad some of what was going on in the organization. Brad could get some things done for them that the managers could not. From both the staff's and managers' perspective, Brad was a powerful and privileged person in the organization, with friends in high places. The leadership reinforced this message by passively permitting and even enabling Brad's behavior. Brad was also a natural leader whom the staff looked to in the absence of leadership from their designated managers. There was undoubtedly something in this arrangement for the leadership: Brad's natural leadership ability, his designated leadership position in the union, and his privileged status with library leaders gave him power to influence staff.

In the short term, Anita's job was to refocus the managers on their performance. She started to help them see their responsibilities concerning Brad's bullying behavior. She also helped them see that they had given their power away, to their own detriment and that of the organization, but that they had choices other than the one they had chosen for so long. Anita coached them to understand the risks and the consequences of the choice they had made and of those other choices available to them. She also helped them learn how to confront Brad through role-playing exercises.

Defining the Issues

The coach's role is to understand and to accurately define or redefine the issues. The coach mentally catalogs her observations over time and analyzes her findings.

Anita mentally backtracked to her initial work with the managers. She jotted notes on the conditions she had encountered in coaching or had observed over the last few months. She arranged these on a white board in relationship to one another: Brad's bullying, the tolerance for Brad's bullying, the intimidation felt by managers, the avoidance of responsibility by the managers and leaders, the credibility gap between staff and managers, the credibility gap between managers and leaders, the ineffectiveness of managers with staff, and the end-running of leadership around ineffective managers.

Anita realized that in attempting to solve one problem, the library's leaders were contributing to another, larger problem. The managers were ineffective in influencing staff to get behind leadership initiatives. The leaders opted to tap into Brad's natural leadership ability. In doing so, they reinforced the status quo: managers could continue to coast, averting their responsibilities, and Brad was allowed to bully others, provided he kept producing for the leadership. Obviously, this manner of doing business would continue to compromise everyone's effectiveness.

Leaders are always teaching, whether they mean to or not. The preceding situation with Brad taught these managers that personalities and not performance mattered to the leadership. To the managers, Brad's belittling and bullying was not appropriate. They had concluded, however, that the leadership preferred Brad to them because of personal, not objective reasons. The leaders, on the other hand, preferred Brad because he could influence staff. They had concluded after several years that the managers were ineffective with staff. Brad's belittling and bullying of staff was a necessary tradeoff, from their perspective.

What might the leadership have done instead? Leaders might have reflected on what they wanted from the managers and coached them. Leaders might have thought about what other stakeholders needed from good managers and how the managers measured up to these expectations. If the leaders had talked with the managers about these expectations, the gap might have been closed between the expectations and each manager's performance. The leaders might have decided to develop those managers who wanted to work up to expectations and to reassign or terminate those who were not so inclined.

The messages leaders send by what they do or don't do, allow or don't allow, have long-term consequences for an organization. They become the unwritten ground rules of the organization and they are absorbed into the organizational culture. They may contradict the spirit of written ground rules: those that are expressed in the organization's statement of values and ethics and in union, civil service, and other agreements, and by what leaders say. Virtually everyone hears the mixed messages and knows there is this double standard.

Double standards and mixed messages confuse and unsettle people. They cannot focus on productive work when they are unsettled about their work environment. Instead, they are fussing about themselves and others in the organization, ever vigilant to rumor and innuendo. They are hopelessly distracted from the important work of the organization.

The Appropriate Coaching Strategy

The coach's role is to develop, deploy, and adjust, as needed, the appropriate short-term and long-term coaching strategies. Once the goals have been defined, the coach must determine an appropriate course of action. (It usually will have multiple dimensions.) The coach imagines a number of possible scenarios. He considers the pros and cons of these, the likelihood of success, the resources that will be invested versus the return on investment, and the consequences for the organization. The coach weighs the possibilities and ultimately makes a judgment about the appropriate strategy or strategies.

- What needs immediate attention?
- What must, can, or should wait?
- What is the likelihood of successfully changing things for the better?
- How long will it take?
- What resources will it take to do so? Are they available?
- What other factors come to bear on this situation?

Anita knew that the library needed an effective management team and that achieving this would require several strategies. Performance expectations for managers needed to be stated, and they must address the needs of all stakeholders, not just those of the leaders. The leaders would also have to clarify their expectations with current managers, and each manager's suitability for coaching must be assessed. Furthermore, the most promising managers would have to be coached into higher levels of performance. Other managers would have to be reassigned or terminated, and any new managers hired must have the skills and abilities to meet the expected performance standards.

Meanwhile, other coaching strategies must involve Brad, staff, the managers, and the leaders. Staff would gradually need to learn that managers would draw the line when it came to Brad's bullying tactics. Brad would need to learn that managers would insist that he observe appropriate standards of conduct. Managers would need to learn how to confront Brad's behavior, how to channel his leadership ability appropriately, and how to help staff regain confidence in them. Leaders would need to be coached about dealing directly with the performance of their managers and about untangling the mixed messages they were sending to staff about performance and accountability.

Performance Barriers and Pathways to Excellence

Just as performance barriers (see figure 1.1) get in the way of individual and team performance, they also can influence the whole organization. Of course, it is only human that these performance barriers will trip us up. A bit of excessive ego here, a little more there—it happens. This is a little barrier. It may temporarily slow down a couple of managers, for instance, each wanting to hire the same person for a vacancy. In the big scheme of things, however, it is not a big deal, provided that the managers quickly regain control of their egos.

Sometimes performance barriers are so pervasive as to seem characteristic of the entire organization. For example, a whole management team with needy egos hurts the team's performance and influences the whole organization that way. In such an organization, individuals throughout the library will tend to be overly focused on self rather than on the team's overall purpose. Performance barriers derail organizations. Little by little, they contribute to the creation of unhealthy conditions. Alternatively, performance pathways, or pathways to excellence (see figure 1.1) lead the way to organizational health and well-being. Coaching guides individuals and teams toward these pathways.

These pathways to excellence influence individual and team performance for the better. Pathways to excellence take the individual, team, and organization toward library excellence, whereas performance barriers obstruct progress on the pathway. Barriers trip us up because they have become pervasive in the organization and create conditions that block individual and team performance.

The role of the coach is to help individuals, teams, leaders, and managers cultivate pathways to excellence. The coach turns people back to these pathways. In the example about Brad, the coach pointed to

- *appropriate boundaries:* the clarification of expectations and roles
- *treating fear:* building the confidence of managers to learn, risk, question, and be responsible

- *doing the right work:* the leadership makes it possible for the managers to learn what they need to know to be effective managers
- *institutional alignment:* the leadership says what it expects of its managers, supports them in their learning, and holds the managers accountable

As leaders cultivate these pathways to excellence, they send clear and consistent messages to managers and staff that

- performance is important
- individuals are also important
- the needs of all the stakeholders matter in this library
- leaders are humane, play fair, and can be trusted to act in good faith

These messages settle staff so they can then gradually shift their focus from fussing and being vigilant to the important work of the library.

WHY COACH FOR ORGANIZATIONAL EFFECTIVENESS?

The primary reason to coach is to focus individuals, teams, and the organization on the library's ultimate purpose: providing excellent service to its community. Staying focused on this ultimate purpose amidst all of the changes libraries are undergoing can be very difficult. With competing demands it is easy to become distracted and discouraged. Yet libraries are on the threshold of being able to revitalize what they provide as institutions and how they operate as organizations. Coaching helps people make the most of this exciting, hopeful, and generative time of change by

- *reintroducing meaningful interaction into the workplace.*
- *improving the quality and consistency of interaction in the workplace.* (Consistency of interaction—not the codification of rules, policies, and procedures—leads to predictability and stability.)
- *promoting employee understanding about where the library is headed and how the individual helps make this possible.* (This understanding generates engagement at the individual level as nothing else can.)

- *contributing to a stable and predictable workplace.* (The more stable and predictable the organization, the safer it is for learning.)
- *actively and willingly supporting people in libraries as they learn by providing feedback and encouragement throughout the learning process.* (Whether the learning has to do with new technology, new skills, or more effective ways of interacting with others to accomplish work, coaching helps people learn.)
- *helping people visualize success.* (For example, a person may be told that her project proposal does not make a convincing case; however, this will not help her understand how to develop a successful project proposal if she thinks she has already done her best. Coaching can help her visualize the desired product.)
- *helping people see possibilities.* (People can become trapped in a pattern of thinking that narrows their range of options. The trusted perspective of another can open their eyes to hidden possibilities, options, and choices. With a little help, people can learn that they can reprogram themselves to deal effectively with the everyday challenges of their work and lives.)
- *helping break isolation.* (What often makes work difficult is that individuals see themselves as alone. They act as if they are solely responsible for coming up with a solution to a challenging or vexing problem and begin to think they are inadequate to the task and that there is no satisfactory solution. They feel trapped under the weight of that isolation. Coaching helps break the isolation, thereby reducing to realistic size burdens that can feel enormous.)
- *helping people cope and adapt.* (A workforce is constantly adjusting or incorporating something new into daily operations. This is now happening in libraries at an accelerated rate.)
- *promoting a workplace counterculture of courage, generosity, positive thinking, confidence, and sufficiency in a dominant work culture that is sometimes inclined toward fear, smallness, negativity, insecurity, and deprivation.*
- *enabling collaborative problem-solving, adaptation, and development of new service, operational, and organizational designs for the library of the future.*

Coaching also helps leaders understand how they influence organizational performance. Consciously or not, leaders profoundly influence organizational effectiveness according to the barriers they impose or reinforce. Likewise, leaders who cultivate pathways to excellence profoundly influence organizational excellence.

Coaching and Change

It bears repeating that people in today's workforce at every level constantly have to work on the interface of their knowledge, skills, and experience in a changing and somewhat unpredictable environment. Coaching by itself will not transform an organization. However, it is a powerful tool in helping individuals and groups in the organization make the transitions that come with change. Change is a constant; it is a catalyst for more change. An organization that understands this and intentionally aids the workforce in making transitions will survive better than one that simply reacts to one change after another. Like scrambling up a pile of tumbling logs, change can be fun and exciting when you are in condition for it.

Many people in libraries are working at the edge, doing things they have never done before, and for which there are no models. They are also having to manage complex social interactions in a more diverse, dynamic workplace. They are dealing with complex workplace issues such as privacy, intellectual freedom, intellectual property, security, and employee liability. The underlying issues may not be new; however, technology has added a new dimension to them.

Many libraries are between order and chaos. They need to be able to constantly organize and reorganize around the work that needs to be done. Work unexpectedly comes bubbling up: learning how to integrate new technology applications, manage a virtual presence, or manage an initiative that does not fit into any box on the organizational chart. Library workers need to design processes, plan projects, and make course corrections quickly and efficiently. They must be able to work well in teams with a more diversely skilled workforce than ever before. They need to be able to shift gears frequently and gracefully to new projects by forming and re-forming teams.

Experts agree that collaboration, teamwork, nimbleness, and resourcefulness are the organizational imperatives of our times. However, many library staff may not be practiced in these ways. Their attention may have been elsewhere and not on building organizational strength and durability for the change that is now upon them. In some libraries, the typical top-down leadership and management styles, organizational models, structures, processes, and the cultural mindsets these changes have fostered have benched many of the players. Under the circumstances, it is no wonder that people are hesitant to get in the game.

For some libraries, competition and defensiveness, rather than collaboration and resourcefulness, characterize their modus operandi. Some are overdeveloped in competing for resources, turf, expertise, space, and recognition. Relationships may be based on competition and conflict: central library versus branches, management versus staff, librarians versus support staff, public services versus technical services, senior staff versus junior staff, you versus me, my idea versus your idea, and on and on. Under the circumstances, how can people in the organization spring over the high jumps of change? They can't, without some help. That's where coaching comes in.

Coaching helps people navigate the dynamic environment that technology has made of libraries. Equally important, coaching helps people learn how to solve problems more efficiently and effectively. It helps build individual and workforce capacity for managing change. With coaching, individuals and teams can rediscover the creativity and fun of work. The chaordic condition of many libraries is full of possibilities and opportunities. It provides a rich field for learning, for creating new methods and models for accomplishing work, and for providing service.

HOW TO COACH FOR ORGANIZATIONAL EFFECTIVENESS

The best way to ensure that the organization achieves and sustains its optimum effectiveness is to cultivate a culture of coaching over time. How can this come about?

Organizations can build their internal capacity to coach. For example, basic coaching skills should be in every manager's tool kit. Organizations can build their internal coaching capacity with classroom instruction and skills practice, shadow coaching,

ongoing workshops, and individual coaching that helps the coach improve his coaching. They can integrate internal and external coaching, accessing the variety of specializations and expertise and building a cadre of coaches who are available as needed.

Organizations can also support the development of coaching skills and behaviors among those who are disposed toward coaching, regardless of their positions. They can develop coaching behaviors in the library director, managers, supervisors, and all staff members. Library leaders can develop their coaching IQ and their coaching capability with direct reports and mentees. They can use coaching to help ensure the success of new hires and of individuals who have been promoted.

Library organizations can integrate coaching with other learning and HR practices, such as training, leadership development, and performance planning and evaluation. They can focus existing organizational resources on addressing performance barriers that are systemic. They can use coaching to develop the organization: to assess its development needs, and to strengthen the individual and collective effectiveness of leadership, management, and cross-functional teams.

Coaches can be hired as employees or contractors to work on staff on a full-time, part-time, or temporary basis. A combination of these approaches can give a library what it needs at any particular point. Furthermore, any of these approaches can be combined with contract coaching on a short-term or long-term basis.

Leaders and managers can use coaching strategically to help individuals and teams navigate the transitions of change. What might these strategies be? They will vary, of course, from organization to organization, based on each organization's self-assessment. What is it that the organization needs to work on to function more effectively? Every library will have its own needs, priorities, resources, and timeline. There is no one-size-fits-all coaching plan, and coaching is not an all-or-nothing proposition. Furthermore, everything does not have to happen at once.

Typically our library organizations need to develop team capability; clarify expectations, roles, responsibilities, and relationships; create models that work for the organization now; explicitly talk about change; learn from and manage conflict; and integrate action learning into individual and team development. These particular strategies are explained below with some examples for illustrative purposes.

Develop team capability. Many people who are used to the hierarchy of libraries find it difficult to actually work in teams. Even those who have no objection to working in teams may not be practiced in teamwork. Typically, people have to be able to function in a traditional hierarchical model and, at other times, to operate in a collaborative team-based model. In fact, they may need to operate in these modes simultaneously. For example, the reference librarian at a large urban library works in the humanities department and reports to a department manager. At the same time, he leads a task force comprised of individuals from various departments across the organization that is charged with recommending an integrated library system.

The coach can help managers start teams well by being explicit about what is to be accomplished. She can be a process coach for the team, observing its initial meetings to help the team get started well. The coach keeps the team on her radar screen, checks in on progress, and helps the team over the humps. The coach can also work with individuals who, though willing to collaborate with others, find it difficult and frustrating. The coach can also help individuals understand, recognize, and comfortably function in various organizational modes.

Clarify expectations, roles, responsibilities, and relationships. One of the most common complaints of library staff is that they do not understand the library's vision and their role in realizing that vision. Library directors, on the other hand, tend to think they are constantly repeating themselves about the library vision and the direction of the library, and that the role of staff is self-evident. Obviously there is a disconnect. The conversation about vision must be ongoing. Things are changing on so many levels so continuously that it is hard for the staff to keep up with the library director and vice versa. Expectations, roles, responsibilities, and relationships are in constant flux. The vision for the library is multifaceted, and the library leader must be constantly interpreting the vision in practical terms, not only for staff but for all of the library's stakeholders: users, taxpayers, governing bodies, elected officials, benefactors, advocates, and adversaries.

The changes that are happening in libraries are confusing; new rules have been added to the game without the accompanying instructions. For exam-ple, some librarians remember when library pages weren't allowed to answer the phone; now library pages are simultaneously taking on leadership roles in the organization. An emergent leader who is a page in the library has been asked by the director to coordinate a cross-functional team on quality improvement. As a page, she reports to the circulation supervisor. As a quality improvement coordinator, she reports to the library director. In a work unit staff meeting, this page is at the lowest rung of the traditional library ladder while simultaneously leading the quality initiative. In her work group, she and not her supervisor may be the expert when it comes to quality improvement. Use a variety of ways to explain these dual, overlapping, and simultaneous modes. Write about them, draw or diagram the relationships, use analogies and metaphors, and give examples and demonstrations. Talk about the expectations and roles. All of these help people understand and adapt more quickly and with less wear and tear on them and others.

Create models that work for the organization now. Help individuals, teams, leaders, and managers be flexible and resourceful in creating ways to organize for the work. Help them see how the level of effort can vary, depending on what the library is trying to accomplish. Show them that there is more than one model for organizing, planning, and processing work and projects—there are many choices, and no single right way to do things. Encourage leaders and managers to regroup by bringing the right people to the table. Help them invent the structures they need for the work at hand. Help them create efficient processes suited to the intended product and learn to trust the process.

Talk about change. People need to talk about change, why it is happening, how it is affecting them, and what it requires of them. Help people understand the change that is happening in the workplace. Just talking about change helps people better cope with it. The following example illustrates one experienced librarian's frustration. This is someone whose mental map of what it means to be a librarian is different from the one that is taking shape in her library.

In a reference staff meeting one day, a frustrated librarian hotly announced to the library director that she and the librarians in her subject reference department were the last remaining stalwart champions of quality reference service. She charged that management neither understood nor cared about quality reference service. "Why else," she asked, "would the leadership suggest that technology training for the public become a routine part of the reference librarian's job? Why else would management be advocating for library assistants to work the reference desk? For over one hundred years, librarians have been the providers of quality reference service, and they have done this from the reference desks of this hallowed institution. To suggest anything other than this is a slap in the face of every professional librarian and a dilution of quality library service."

Learn from and manage conflict. The tendency in many organizations is to shy away from conflict. Instead, listen and manage conflict well. There is a great deal to learn from listening to people when they are upset. Furthermore, applying coaching skills to these situations models how to process conflict. Applying the skills of the coach shows others how to have difficult conversations. This is how people learn that there is life after conflict: situation by situation, day in and day out. Without the supporting dialogue about change, people who are angry about change remain angry. Expressed frustrations such as the one in the preceding example are really opportunities that open the door for dialogue and understanding. The coach can guide this outburst, for example, into a dialogue about the evolving role of the librarian. The frustrated librarian may not like the change, but at least she has the opportunity to hear from leaders, managers, and fellow staff about what these changes mean to them. This broader perspective may influence a more hopeful, opportunistic view for this librarian than was reflected in her remarks. With the skills of a coach, people learn that they can move from anger into meaningful interaction.

Integrate action learning into individual and team development. Act on the premise that the need to learn new skills and practices in today's library is a given for everyone at every level of the organization. Help others understand that this is also an opportunity for individual self-development and organizational development. Use opportunities for action learning. Action learning puts people to work on what the organization needs by being involved in the work, with the intention of learning new skills, processes, and behaviors. Action learning is supported by coaching. Coaching helps the learners reflect on the experience and learn from it.

For instance:

After a few years of downsizing the staff, a library needed to hire many new employees quickly to staff newly funded library hours. The personnel department was small, and the hiring process was labor-intensive. The department staff knew it could not accomplish the requisite scale of hiring and do it well without help. They enlisted dozens of staff throughout the library to hire, orient, and train the new employees. This not only worked, it was also exciting for everyone involved. Individuals for whom the hiring process had been a mystery learned what it entailed and why. Rank-and-file staff had input into the selection of professional and managerial staff for the first time in the library's history. They also helped orient and train many new staff, refreshing their own knowledge in the process and learning how to train others. New interview models that emerged were retained because they worked better for the library than the old models.

Was this the best, most efficient, most economical way to hire for the library? No one can know for sure, but one thing is certain: Everyone involved was proud of what they had accomplished together and of what they had learned about the organization. Furthermore, the library reinvented its hiring process. In the library lore of this particular institution, this was one of its greatest success stories.

Help develop institutional patience for skill building, individual development, and behavioral changes. At times, progress may need to be slowed while learners catch up. Expect learning to temporarily slow down production. Assume that this will improve over time, and advocate that others give learning a chance.

Just about anywhere you think coaching should begin is a good place to start. For example, it may be that the director wants executive coaching or that a manager needs help with a particular problem in one of her units. It might be that the management team is stalled, the technology committee is floundering, or the library needs a critical mass of coaching to focus on a particular condition in the organization. Whatever the need, the main thing is that leaders and managers see it, acknowledge it, and purposefully address it. That is how coaching for organizational effectiveness begins.

This chapter addressed how systemic barriers can impede organizational effectiveness. The application that follows is a classic example. As you have seen, all coaching doesn't look the same. This particular vignette illustrates how handling a seemingly isolated situation has implications for the whole organization. In this application, you will witness the coaching dialogue that helps the player resolve her dilemma.

APPLICATION

FOCUSING ON ORGANIZATIONAL EFFECTIVENESS

Background

Don is awaiting a disciplinary decision from management for his involvement in the loss of several thousand dollars' worth of library books. He had "borrowed" the books, he said, including several from the rare book collection. He had then loaned them to a friend who was conducting research and who had promised to return the books to Don. Now Don could not locate the friend or the books.

Don had admitted to borrowing the books when his supervisor, Marty, first confronted him. However, Don had said he would get them back immediately. Not only had he failed to do so, but he also had not been forthcoming with Marty in disclosing the scale of his "borrowing." Instead, Marty had had to extract over several days the details of what was taken and the related incidents and alleged circumstances that, even now, he could not be confident were complete or true.

Marty felt Don's piecemeal story simply did not hang together. However, Marty had reached the point of realizing that getting the whole truth and the full account was secondary to addressing Don's continuing presence in the library. Marty had lost all confidence in Don's trustworthiness and judgment. As Don's supervisor, Marty was responsible for taking this matter to the library's personnel manager, Leanna.

Don insisted that he had been a victim of his friend. Furthermore, he seemed wounded that Marty had characterized the incident as stealing. Don alleged that this manner of borrowing books by staff was common practice, and he thought management knew about it.

Don claimed that he had not disclosed the full list of books or made a full account of the incidents because he didn't realize that was what Marty was asking of him.

Don insisted that for nearly four years he had been a trustworthy employee and that his victimization should be taken into account by management in determining if there would be any disciplinary action. Don appealed to his union; he brought a union representative to the prediscipline hearing. He said he was sorry for all the trouble he had caused. However, he claimed that he could not see that he had done anything to warrant the continuing mistrust of Marty. Under the circumstances, Don said his conduct was understandable and certainly did not warrant his dismissal.

In meetings with Marty, and later with Marty and Leanna, Don contradicted himself in answering questions about the relevant events. He frequently responded to questions concerning his actions and decisions with "I don't know," "I don't recall," or "I don't remember." Consciously or not, Don played on Marty's and Leanna's sympathies, making reference to his alcohol recovery efforts and repeatedly saying that he did not want exceptional treatment because of his difficult personal circumstances.

The issue for Leanna, with input from Marty, was to recommend to the library director the appropriate disciplinary action. The library policies and union contract stipulated the disciplinary process and the range of options. The question in this case was whether to recommend a period of suspension without pay or to terminate Don's employment.

(continued)

Leanna must base her decision, among other things, on the library's past practice in similar situations. Personnel rules and contract stipulations allowed for consideration of extenuating circumstances. She must also consider the practical, legal, and political consequences of the decision.

Foremost in Leanna's mind were the possible ramifications of disciplining an employee who was enrolled in an alcohol treatment program. She was concerned that if Don lost his job, he or his union representative or future legal counsel might claim that he had been discriminated against on the basis of a health condition.

On a personal level, Leanna was also concerned that the loss of his job might undo Don's recovery and jeopardize his well-being and that of his children. She knew that Don was a single parent and that his addiction had once nearly lost him custody of his children. She knew that what Don did was wrong, but she was concerned about the hardship on Don and his children if he was out of a job. Leanna thought that the more lenient suspension would be less risky for the library and for Don.

After extensive discussions, Marty and Leanna were at odds about the recommendation. Marty firmly believed that Don should be dismissed from employment, while Leanna favored suspension.

Marty asserted, "I cannot trust Don. Whatever actually happened here, we may never know. I do know that I will be constantly looking over my shoulder to watch Don, worried that he may be stealing from the library. Furthermore, how can I trust his judgment? He believes he has done nothing wrong. If he can't see his responsibility in this, how can I count on him to act responsibly?"

The authority for the recommendation was Leanna's. However, she respected Marty and did not want to put him in the position of having to police Don. Still, she felt that the personal extenuating circumstances and the potential ramifications for the library justified a more lenient action. The library hadn't actually had a parallel situation, but in the few cases of theft

of property or money, the offending employees had resigned because the facts were so compelling. There was no precedent in the library's disciplinary history for a situation like this.

Leanna felt she was on the horns of a dilemma. She asked Dana, a peer manager whom she respected, to meet with and to coach her by reviewing her reasoning and providing an objective perspective. Dana met with Leanna and listened to a recap of the case, asked clarifying questions, and verified her role in this matter.

The Coaching Dialogue

Dana said, "My role, as I understand it, is to help you resolve your dilemma about one of two possible choices concerning Don: suspension or termination. Is that correct?"

"Yes, that's right," Leanna replied.

Dana went on, "In listening to the review of this case, Leanna, I surmise that you favor the suspension because you believe it's a more lenient decision. Tell me why you favor leniency for Don."

Leanna replied, "Well, essentially for two reasons. First, I think it is less risky for the library. I think Don could claim that being terminated is related to his alcoholism. Legally, this could be a problem for the library. Second, as the personnel manager, I'm concerned about putting Don out of a job. I worry about what that might do to his recovery and I worry about the effect on his children. I know that Don has struggled as a single parent, and I can relate to that. I know that Don had been on the verge of homelessness when he came to the library four years ago."

Dana thought about this, and then said, "Let's talk about the first reason, Leanna. It occurs to me that Don could make the claim that either disciplinary action was related to his alcoholism. Yet you are not conflicted about suspending him. Why is that?"

Leanna replied, "What Don did was wrong, and I have no problem with the library making that point. I think the suspension would do that. However, termination is more drastic, and that is what could put us at risk."

Dana continued, "And the risk is that Don may claim that his termination is related to his alcoholism. Would he be right?"

Immediately, Leanna replied, "Of course not. This isn't about his alcoholism. It is about his dishonesty."

Dana continued, "And if Don or a representative should make a legal claim—challenge either decision on that basis—do you think the library could make a solid case in defense of itself, given the documentation you and Marty have from your investigation?"

Leanna nodded. "Yes, I do. But the courts might not see it that way."

Dana sat back. "We're still talking about your first reason for favoring the suspension, but I want to shift now from talking about Don to talking about Marty. Do you believe that suspending Don will restore Marty's trust in Don?"

Leanna thought this over, and then replied, "No, I don't. I don't blame Marty for feeling this way, because I don't trust Don, either. For whatever reason, Don is just not making good decisions. Marty will have to be watching Don, and he won't be able to believe what Don says. I hate to put Marty in that position, which is why I asked for your help."

Switching points, Dana said, "Let's talk about the second reason you favor suspension, Leanna. You said you are worried about Don and about his children—that a decision you make will precipitate negative consequences for Don and his children and you don't want to be responsible for precipitating such consequences. Leanna, it strikes me that your worry about Don is what has you on the horns of a dilemma.

"I say that because you really have the risk concern covered. You have said that Don was wrong in what he did and that suspending him will not make him trustworthy. You have said that while there is a risk that Don will legally challenge the basis for either decision, you have solid documentation to make the case that the discipline had to do with Don's performance and not his alcoholism. It seems to me that you really do know that the risk is greater to the library to retain Don than it is to terminate him. What do you think about what I have just said?"

Leanna considered this and said, "I think you're right about the risk issue. There's a greater probability, I suppose, that Don will compromise the library again than there is that the library would be legally challenged—and

still less of a risk that a legal challenge would be upheld. So the greater risk to the library is in keeping Don employed here. My dilemma is, then, about what happens to Don as a result of losing his job. I know in my head that that is not my responsibility. However, my heart doesn't agree. It feels inhumane to cut Don loose without any notice. I don't want us to be that kind of library. What will he do to keep a roof over his head and food on the table? That's what I'm struggling with."

Dana smiled. "Maybe there is something you could do, Leanna, to make the termination as humane as possible, something that is in your control."

Puzzled, Leanna said, "What do you mean? I don't understand."

Dana explained, "You believe the library values being humane and you want to express that to Don. What are ways that you can do that, on behalf of the library, that are within the boundaries of your or the director's authority?

"For example, you feel it is inhumane to cut Don loose without notice. Are you authorized to recommend paid administrative leave for a reasonable time, prior to the effective date of the termination?"

Slowly Leanna smiled. "Yes, actually, I could recommend to the director two weeks of paid administrative leave followed by termination. That seems justified to me because we will require Don to vacate the premises immediately following our telling him our decision. This is a security precaution and standard practice when someone leaves under similar circumstances. Two weeks would give Don at least some margin of time to find another job. I'd feel better if the library could do that."

Dana's smile broadened as she said, "Good. It occurs to me that another way to be humane is to communicate to Don that this was a difficult decision and perhaps to succinctly say why the decision went this way. The point of doing so is not to defend the decision but to let Don hear that this is about his behavior, not about who he is."

Leanna nodded and said, "Yes, and I also think we can encourage Don, if he expresses discouragement about his future employability, by reminding him of the skills he has and has developed at the library."

(continued)

Dana approvingly said, "That's the idea, Leanna. You can give this more thought and talk it over with the director when you meet to inform him of your recommendation."

How is this vignette about organizational effectiveness? Had the personnel manager's decision taken its initial course, the message it would send throughout the organization would certainly have seemed to contradict library policies. This doesn't have to happen many times before the stability of staff is undermined. It sends mixed messages to employees, and this is confusing and upsetting—and undermines confidence in the organization's leadership.

Library policies are useful boundaries that help large numbers of people understand how to operate within the organization. They are community standards of conduct that people agree to respect when they come to work in that organization. Such standards are common in any community of people, and they are a frame of reference for conducting oneself in that particular community. When someone violates those boundaries, as did Don, all heads turn to see if the community standard is being upheld. Employees also look to see that their fellow workers are treated fairly and humanely.

It is only human to be saddened at times by the circumstances of people's lives. However, letting this be the basis for our decisions can undercut our responsibilities to the library. In this case, the manager must keep in mind that Don is not a patient; he is an employee. It is possible to be sympathetic to a problem without trying to solve that problem if it is beyond our control.

Situations like Don's call for the manager to remain steady on course for the library. Employees want to see that the organization acts responsibly. The decision maker must be ever mindful of what is helpful for the entire range of people in the organization. The employer in this case gave Don a fair and humane hearing and an honest and responsible decision for the good of the library. In the end, the personnel manager's recommendation reinforced the library's values and sent a consistent message to staff.

conclusion

THE MOST important lesson to take away from this book is that coaching is a multifaceted, multidimensional tool for creating and sustaining truly effective organizations. The survival of libraries is as much a consequence of adaptable, flexible, and durable organizations as it is a matter of adapting services to an ever-changing marketplace. These are two sides of the same coin. You don't get one without the other.

Coaching is much more than problem-solving. In the last decade, it has become more accessible and ubiquitous across the globe. Leaders are creating cultures of coaching, integrating coaching in its many forms into their organizations. Doing so has become a new standard by which leadership performance is measured.

It is time for library leaders to seriously address building the internal muscle of their library organizations, and coaching is a tool that will aid them. Coaching is not just for problem-solving but for preparing the organization to adapt to an ever-changing environment. Creating and sustaining such organizations is not an accident but is the result of thoughtful, strategic, and sustained commitment by library leaders.

It is time to become purposeful about the application of coaching in libraries on a broad scale. Library leaders can authorize and influence the development of a "coaching system" in their organizations that supports the learning and development of individuals and the organization as a whole. A coaching system can in turn be integrated into ongoing "systems" such as learning, performance management, and leadership development.

Coaching by itself will not transform an organization. However, it is a powerful tool in helping individuals and groups in the organization make the transitions that come with change. Change is a constant; it is a catalyst for more change. An organization that understands this and intentionally aids the workforce in making transitions will survive better than one that simply reacts to one change after another.

Some of the concepts in this book will apply to your organization while others will not. Every library will have its own needs, priorities, resources, and timeline. There is no one-size-fits-all coaching plan, and coaching is not an all-or-nothing proposition. Furthermore, everything does not have to happen at once. Coaching does not have to be difficult or expensive, and each library can start at its point of need. Coaching is not the answer to everything, but it is an important and proven tool in creating the kind of work environment that is helping enterprises from every sector meet the demands of a constantly changing world.

Coaching actively and willingly supports people in libraries as they learn. It is, after all, our consistency of interaction in the face of constant change that leads to stability, predictability, and a more durable workplace. This durability gives people a firm place to stand, even amidst constant change. It is the ultimate place from which to be consistently effective as an organization and community institution.

selected resources

THERE HAS BEEN been a proliferation of resources on coaching in recent years. This list of best resources is a guide for the busy library person.

CONTACTING THE AUTHOR

For people who want to pursue coaching, Ruth Metz is happy to respond to actual scenarios or to help libraries find library coaches that suit their needs. Ruth likes to hear from fellow coaches, too. You can get in touch with the author at www.library coach.com. Through coaching, consulting, and training, Ruth helps clients develop their organizations. She coaches library directors, managers, and library leadership teams. She helps organizations develop a coaching culture in their organizations by training coaches to coach and mentors to mentor.

THE BASICS

If you are someone who wants to learn how to coach or to improve your coaching, these basic resources will be very useful.

Brounstein, Marty. *Coaching and Mentoring for Dummies.* New York: Hungry Minds, 2000.
Written in an easy style, this book can help managers learn how to be better coaches through giving feedback in a positive way, motivating employees, and dealing effectively with diversity issues, performance reviews, and other challenges.

Kinlaw, Dennis C. *Coaching for Commitment: Interpersonal Strategies for Obtaining Superior Performance from Individuals and Teams.* 2nd edition. San Francisco: Jossey-Bass Pfeiffer, 1999.
Kinlaw's book is very straightforward and easy to follow. The book presents a generic treatment of coaching rather than one imbedded in a corporate or business context.

Kinlaw explains what coaching is and provides a basic structure. Readers will find his coaching dialogues useful and illustrative. He provides two coaching process models that new and experienced coaches will find useful and does a good job of describing the core skills of the coach. The book also includes a chapter on coaching teams and another on self-development of the coach.

Dotlich, David L. *Action Coaching: How to Leverage Individual Performance for Company Success*. San Francisco: Jossey-Bass, 1999.
With its corporate-sounding title, this book may turn some away. However, what makes it different from most others is that it emphasizes coaching as an organizational intervention, when new behaviors are brought in at the moment the organization most needs them—the moment of difficulty. It includes some tools for matching coaches with employees. Action coaching involves a series of steps and some specific coaching tools. This book is recommended for those who are new to training and development, or for employees who are considering getting coached.

Perry Zeus and Suzanne Skiffington have written three books together on coaching, all of which are very useful. Both authors have been in the business of professional coaching since the early 1990s. These authors refer to coaching as "the new technology of learning and change." They have written *The Complete Guide to Coaching at Work* (2000), *The Coaching at Work Toolkit: A Complete Guide to Techniques and Practices* (2002), and *Behavioral Coaching: How to Build Sustainable Personal and Organizational Strength* (2005), all published by McGraw-Hill. Zeus has also written many articles on coaching. He lectures, mentors a small, select group of CEOs, and leads coaching research. He is the chair of the board of directors of the Behavioral Coaching Institute, with which he and Skiffington are affiliated. Their books are best-selling coaching textbooks that are clearly and concisely written, with examples and tools for the coach. For example, *The Coaching at Work Toolkit* includes a variety of "profile" questionnaires that can be used for assessing various coaching situations.

LEADER COACH

As stated in the introduction to this book, many organizations today expect their executives to be "leader coaches" and to develop coaching throughout their organizations. The best one-volume resource for this is *The CCL Handbook of Coaching: A Guide for the Leader Coach,* edited by Sharon Ting and Peter Scisco. It is a joint publication of the Jossey-Bass business and management service and the Center for Creative Leadership, 2006.

The Center for Creative Leadership (CCL) is a nonprofit educational institution with an international reach. Its mission is to advance the understanding, practice, and development of leadership for the benefit of society worldwide. The CCL is based in Greensboro, North Carolina. It conducts research, produces publications and assessment tools, and offers educational programs.

The *CCL Handbook* is not a quick read for the leader who is coaching others. However, it is a useful one-source overview of coaching for leadership development. In that respect, it is an especially useful tool for library directors and HR units for its research-enriched perspective and the included CD-ROM library of classic CCL publications. In one source, it provides an overview of the foundations of leadership coaching and speaks to the most important issues in leadership development and leadership coaching, including "Coaching for Specific Leadership Challenges and Capacities," "Coaching for Special Populations," and "Extending the Coaching Practice" into the organization.

COACHING FOR SPECIAL POPULATIONS

Bacon, Terry R., and Karen I. Spear. *Adaptive Coaching: The Art and Practice of a Client-Centered Approach to Performance Improvement*. Mountain View, CA: Davies-Black, 2003.
This book is especially useful for its section on coaching special populations. Reading it will increase one's awareness of one's own limited perspective when coaching someone from a different culture, status, gender, age, or race. Bacon and Spear offer great insights on how to be more aware, sensitive, and effective in coaching people with significantly different backgrounds from that of the coach.

The *CCL Handbook on Coaching* referenced above also has a useful section on coaching for special populations. It speaks to cross-cultural issues, coaching women leaders, and coaching leaders of color. CCL treats senior leaders as a special population, too, because coaching them is typically different from coaching managers below the top level. These people have special coaching needs because of their unique roles, positions of influence, and broad scope of responsibility.

WHERE TO FIND A COACH

The introduction to *Coaching in the Library* maintains that a thoughtful defining of the coaching need is the first step in selecting the right coach. Next, sleuthing by way of colleagues may be the best way, for now, to begin to look for a coach for your purposes.

This may seem a parochial approach. However, there is a kind of crisis of accountability in coaching stemming from the lack of rigor in coaching standards, and the absence of an accepted standard for measuring the results of coaching. Until this improves, the search for a coach is best begun by talking with trusted people in your network of associates. Your network includes peers in other libraries, library association committees, consortia, and so forth. It probably also includes community, business, governmental, and educational peers. You may also have established relationships with management consultants who could be a source of referral.

In concert with doing some initial groundwork with your trusted network, you can also refer to library consultant-finding sources. At the present time, only the libraryconsultants.org website lists library coaches, per se. In other library consultants lists, you can look under headings like "management" to search for coaches. These include directories published by the American Library Association and its divisions: the Special Library Association and the Library Leadership and Management Association.

Library Consultants Directory Online, www.libraryconsultants.org.
This database of library industry consultants can be searched by name, area of expertise, or geographic region. Coaching is explicitly listed. Search other subject areas as appropriate, such as management, staff development and training, leadership development, organizational development, team development, and recruitment and retention.

The exponentially growing coaching industry has coach-finding services which differ in qual-

ity. If you go this route, try the Behavioral Coach Institute first because following your initial inquiry online, you get a phone call back to discuss your needs without a fee.

Behavioral Coach Institute.
Founded by authors Zeus and Skiffington noted above, this organization claims to provide a number of coaching services for organizations, including various coaching and mentoring certification courses, clinics, and specialty coaching workshops. If your library has a coaching program, they will evaluate it. For this online coach referral, visit www.1to1coachingschool.com.

The International Coach Federation also has an online directory you can search by type of coaching, name, and geographic location.

International Coach Federation, www.coachfederation.com/ethics.htm.
Formed in 1995, this appears to be the largest international coaching organization, with over 16,000 members. It is a nonprofit organization with members in over ninety countries. The federation's website, though fairly sparse in content, includes a coaching code of ethics and standards of conduct. The online coach referral service as of this writing does not include libraries, government, or nonprofit listings. Coach groupings are corporate, small business, personal, and career. Library leaders looking for coaches would start with the corporate category and choose one or more subcategories as well as by locale.

Of course, you can use the online coaching referral services for your coach-finding: to check professional credentials, specialties, and proximity of the coach to your library. However, don't rely on these services without exercising the same rigor you would use for hiring any professional to provide a service to your library.

COACHING WORKSHOPS AND CLASSES

A limited amount of exposure to coaching "training" is available from the library industry in person, online, or both.

For the library person who is looking for an introduction to coaching or to better understand how to coach as a supervisor, manager, or leader, these resources will be useful.

The SirsiDynix Institute is an ongoing forum for professional development in the library community. The institute provides access to industry-leading speakers through its free web seminars. The Dynix Institute has featured coaching in its web seminars for several years. Sessions are archived and searchable at www.sirsidynixinstitute.com.

InfoPeople, California's training gateway, has held half-day and full-day workshops throughout California on coaching and related topics over the past several years. These sessions are open to library people outside of California for a fee. The website posts workshops, and the session materials are archived online and available for self-study to anyone.

The Association of Research Libraries, Office of Leadership and Management Services, offers an online coaching course at www.arl.org/training/coaching.html. The course is offered in collaboration with Southern Illinois University, Carbondale, Library Affairs, Instructional Support Services. This is a good, basic course in coaching that will benefit the novice and the seasoned supervisor.

Coaching industry certification programs offer training and continuing education related to becoming certified as a coach. For these latter programs, check the websites of the Peer Resources Network, cited below, and the International Coach Federation and the Behavioral Coach Institute, both cited above.

BEST PLACE TO KEEP LOOKING

If you haven't found what you are looking for in this "Selected Resources" list, the single best source for books, articles, audiovisual materials, instruction and certification, and other coaching resources is the Peer Resources Network (www.peer.ca/profile.html).

Peer Resources has been in operation as a nonprofit educational corporation since 1975. It claims to have an unequaled record of experienced and published experts in peer, mentor, and coach systems in Canada. Its mission is to provide high-quality training, superior educational resources, and practical consultation. The website includes an index to coaching schools, coaching services, certification, coaches, and all manner of coaching resources.

The world of coaching is changing daily. This "Selected Resources" list will be helpful but outdated by the time it is published. More and more opportunities will become available for online instruction and finding sources. The author maintains a "Best Resources" list on her website, www.librarycoach.com. She also helps library organizations locate coaches for their specific needs.

index

You may also be interested in

BE A GREAT BOSS: ONE YEAR TO SUCCESS
Catherine Hakala-Ausperk

To help library managers improve their skills and acumen, renowned speaker and trainer Catherine Hakala-Ausperk presents a handy self-study guide to the dynamic role of being a boss. This workbook is organized in 52 modules, designed to cover a year of weekly sessions but easily adaptable for any pace.

ISBN: 978-0-8389-1068-9 / 232 PGS / 8.5" × 11"

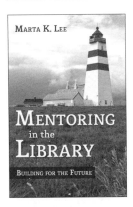

MENTORING IN THE LIBRARY: BUILDING FOR THE FUTURE
Marta K. Lee

Noted reference librarian and researcher Marta K. Lee offers librarians at all levels both her experience and her ideas about establishing a formal mentoring process at the library.

ISBN: 978-0-8389-3593-4 / 136 PGS / 6" × 9"

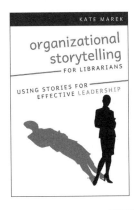

ORGANIZATIONAL STORYTELLING FOR LIBRARIANS: USING STORIES FOR EFFECTIVE LEADERSHIP
Kate Marek

Just as literature can be used for learning, the power of storytelling can be very effective when applied to leadership. Applying solid management principles to a library setting, Kate Marek provides the tools and explains the process of leading and managing through organizational storytelling.

ISBN: 978-0-8389-1079-5 / 120 PGS / 6" × 9"

MANAGING LIBRARY VOLUNTEERS, SECOND EDITION
Preston Driggers and Eileen Dumas

Quality volunteers can make a world of difference in today's library, and this hands-on guide gives you everything you need to maximize your library's services and build a bridge between your library and the community it serves.

ISBN: 978-0-8389-1064-1 / 323 PGS / 8.5" × 11"

Order today at alastore.ala.org or 866-746-7252!
ALA Store purchases fund advocacy, awareness, and accreditation programs for library professionals worldwide.